Head Winds

Head Winds

by: Willy L. Warbelow

*Great Northwest Publishing
and Distributing Company, Inc.*
Anchorage, Alaska
1987

With my deepest love, I dedicate this story to our children, Cyndie, Ron, Charlie, and Art, who were always there to support us through the bad times and the good.

ACKNOWLEDGEMENTS

Dr. Charles Keim — Guidance, advice, and encouragement
Carol Wallace Warbelow — Typing manuscript
Hazel Bodette — Papers and letters covering period 1948-1970

People who furnished pictures:
Helen Foster — Palo Alto, Calif.
Robert Carroll — Inverness, Florida
Everette and Buela Castoe — Townsend, Tenn.
Carl Charles — Dot Lake, Alaska
Robert Stonoff — Tempe, Arizona
Mary Glidden Roberts — Tok, Alaska
Steve Leriget — Fairbanks, Alaska
Ron Warbelow — Tok, Alaska
Cyndie Warbelow Tack — Two Rivers, Alaska
Roger Norris — Bloomer, Wisconsin
Frank and Fern Baehm — Yakima, Washington
Anderson Bakewell, S.J. — Sante Fe, New Mexico

People who gave me technical or general information:
Helen Foster — Palo Alto, Calif.
John Erickson — Tok, Alaska
K.C. Jones — Tok, Alaska
Lavell Wilson — Tok, Alaska
Ray Mathews — Tok, Alaska
Nelson Walker — Kotzebue, Alaska
Betty Smith — Delta Junction, Alaska
Corky Sager — Sequim, Washington

FOREWORD

In the fall of 1945 at the close of World War II, Marvin and Willy Lou Warbelow, as newly weds, left Wisconsin to teach in the Eskimo villages of Artic Alaska. Three years later Marvin brought his first plane north to the Territory with him, and thus began his 22-year love affair with airplanes and flying. He soon joined the ranks of Alaska's genuine bush pilots.

Over the years, as they moved from village to village, and as their family grew to a daughter and three sons, there was always an airplane in the family.

In 1956 the Warbelows gave up their teaching and opened a roadhouse and air service on the Alaska Highway. Because Alaska was still a real frontier, the airplane was an essential part of the way of life; and because the country still lacked sufficient airstrips, bush pilots had to do a lot of improvising. Landings were made on river bars, beaches, roads, and any other reasonably clear areas. Skill, knowledge of the country, and nerves of steel were required for survival.

The Warbelows not only survived, but thrived on the rigorous and challenging life along the Alaska Highway. Their roadhouse, Cathedral Bluffs, became an outpost (25 miles from their nearest neighbors) around which all kinds of activity revolved. Accident victims were airlifted to hospitals, hunters and trappers (even their dogs) were flown to remote areas in quest of game, miners and prospectors were supplied and looked for promising new lodes by air, mail and supplies were regularly delivered to the "bush", and geologists, biologists, and other scientists were supported in their work. The whole family was involved in "keeping Marvin flying."

As the children grew older their responsibilities increased and airplanes were refueled between school lessons (at home by correspondence). Willy Lou not only ran the roadhouse, cooking, cleaning and entertaining of tourists with stories of life in the Arctic, but also hauled aviation fuel from Tok by truck, saw that airplanes were properly tied down when Marvin was out flying, kept impatient hunters and prospectors who were waiting for flights fed and amused, hauled mail from post-office to airplane, gassed cars of "locals" and tourists, kept track of messages and flights, and was mother and school teacher for four children.

Marvin was not only a legendary bush pilot, but a father, a teacher, and mainstay of the community. He could fix almost anything and could come up with ingenious ways to get float planes in and out of the water or do other difficult tasks with limited equipment. He could render first aid or help with a bookkeeping problem. Politics and local and world problems were commonly discussed over late night coffee and pie at the cafe counter at Cathedral Bluffs, and Marvin's advice was often sought on everything from "soup to nuts".

The Warbelows and Cathedral Bluffs became an institution, the heart of which was Marvin's intrepid bush flying, aided by his ground crew, Willy Lou and the children. Now, Willy Lou Warbelow Young accurately and picturesquely describes a unique and colorful episode in the history of Alaska's "growing up."

Helen Foster
U.S. Geological Survey

MARVIN WARBELOW
AN APPRECIATION

When Willy Lou called me to say she was in the process of writing a book about Marvin I was surprised and happy, Marvin needs a book to bring to light some of his astounding accomplishments. These were done in a matter of fact way, as if there was nothing unusual about them. But the fact is, his life was full of unusual accomplishments, for he was a most unusual man, though he would be the last to admit it.

In the autumn of 1967 I was given an assignment: the care of the Eastern flank of Alaska. The area involved stretched from the Alaska Range in the South to the Yukon River in the North, and from the Delta River Eastward to the border of the Yukon Territory. This comprised about 35,000 square miles. I was the only priest to care for it. The chaplain at Fort Greely took care of his troops at the Northern Warfare Training Center, leaving the rest to me. Under the circumstances, I cast about for a bit of help, and found it in Marvin and his boys. In the course of the next nine years we did a lot of flying together: crisscrossing the Forty Mile Country, dropping in on Eagle, Boundary, Chisana, Tok, Northway, Tanacross, and God only knows how many desolate gravel bars, unnamed lakes and rock strewn ridges. Whatever it was, Marvin and his boys, were ready. Not only were they ready, they did each job remarkably well, and with no fuss.

The weather and the terrain left very little margin for human error. "There are old pilots, and there are bold pilots. But there are *no* old, bolt pilots." I have seen my own thermometer drop to 80 F below zero. As I was not a certified weather observer (as I was in the Himalayas) this record was not official. But there it was: a hundred and twelve degrees below freezing. The landscape varied from 13,000 feet peaks to glaciers, rivers, tundra and low rolling hills. None of it made much difference to Marvin. He took it all in stride. He would *never* elaborate upon the occasional (and inevitable to anyone flying that country) mishaps. He could not quite make it off a gravel bar once, hit the water and the plane nosed into the river. He and the geologist took a couple of days to walk out along the ridges of the Forty Mile Country. When I asked him about it later he said quite simply: "dinged a prop." That was the end of it. His sons learned from him to improvise. Once in the Robertson River a flying stone bent Ron's prop on landing. When help was slow acoming he took a rock, banged the propeller straight and took off. The torque was bad, but he made it.

One time in a wild and lonely river bar, Marvin left me to make an eight day Retreat. When he came in after the third day I knew something was wrong. "Your father is dead" was all he said. We broke camp and flew in. "For this trip" he said "there is no charge."

The death of any great man leaves an awful gap. Marvin's sons filled it, and filled it well. I am proud of them, and you will be when you read this book. They are true sons of a grand pilot and a valiant woman.

Anderson Bakewell, S.J.
Santa Fe, New Mexico 1987

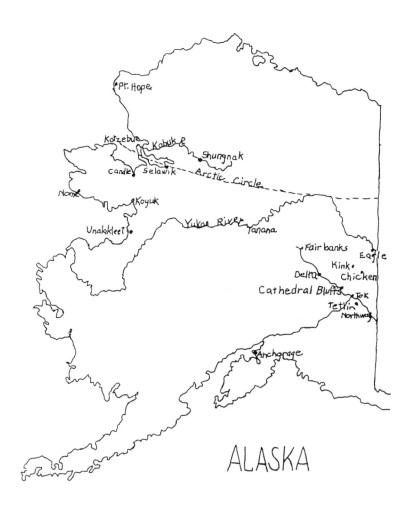

Pt. Hope

Kotzebue
Kobuk R.
Shungnak
candle
Selawik
Arctic Circle

Nome

Koyuk

Yukon River
Tanana

Unalakleet

Fairbanks
Eagle
Kink
Chicken
Delta
Cathedral Bluffs
Tok
Tetlin
Northway

Anchorage

ALASKA

Marvin never allowed anything to come easy for himself. He spent most of his life bucking head winds.

CHAPTER I

"Why are you slowing up?"

"I'm going to pull up on this straight stretch here. I want to talk to you, Lou."

"Can't you talk without stopping the car?" I asked.

Marvin didn't answer. He pulled to the side of the road, and turned off the switch.

"Lou," he said flatly, "maybe I should quit. I don't think I can ever learn to fly that airplane."

"What's wrong," I asked. "What makes you think you can't fly it?"

"Well, it's these stalls. I've been working at them for three lessons now, and I've made no progress at all."

"But you've only taken six hours of lessons. Maybe you aren't supposed to know how to do them yet."

"Yes, I am," he insisted. "I'm thinking about all the guys I've heard make the remark that they took a few flying lessons — five or six — but they quit. Now I know why. It's on those fifth and sixth hours where you start stalls, and it's probably what stopped them."

I was getting a little perturbed. "Listen, Marvin," I reminded him. "I think you're forgetting something. You *can't* quit.

15

Remember, you've already bought the airplane!''

And so he had.

We were back in northern Wisconsin for the summer with my sister's family near Boyceville, after almost three years of teaching in an Eskimo village in arctic Alaska. It was an action-packed summer for us. Our first child was due in a month, and that was already beginning to be a full-time job for me. But Marvin had two projects on hand. He was going to summer school in Superior, 160 miles north of us. And on weekends he was down in Durand, 40 miles to the south, taking flight lessons. He had made a deal with Clarence Schlosser, his instructor. For $1250, Clarence sold him a Piper J5 plane and guaranteed him a private pilot's license. There had been no agreement made as to what the plane was worth and what the lessons were worth. It just wasn't a package that could be split up.

We mulled over the pros and cons, and talked about the high hopes he had built up of returning to Alaska with his own plane.

"You know," I reminded him, "you promised me you wouldn't take a new baby back to the Arctic without a plane at our front door just in case it had to get to a doctor."

"I know. I know. Tell you what we'll do. This is Saturday. I've got one more day of lessons before I have to go back to school. We'll try it tomorrow. If things aren't better then, there's no use."

That day was all he needed. He conquered the stalls, and in the next 22 years he logged 12,000 hours.

CHAPTER II

The stalls might have been a problem, but they were only the beginning. Marvin was no kid. He was already 32 years old and had no background for flying at all. but you couldn't live in Alaska, and especially in the arctic, without rubbing elbows with the fellows who flew; and eventually you had to get the bug. Every visitor who stopped in our village came by plane, and the pilot usually stood by for his passengers. So of course the conversation leaned heavily toward planes, flying weather, and the personal predicaments that every old bush pilot loved to relate.

Marvin had logged ten and a half hours before Clarence finally, at the end of a successful landing on June 26, crawled out of the plane, and in his easy-going way said, "All right. Take it off by yourself now."

Three days later, when Cyndie, our new daughter, was just five days old, Marvin circled the hospital a few times, just to let me and everyone else in the building know he was up there, and to "get the kid used to the sound of the plane."

The J5 was a colorful little character. Bright orange on the outside, it was a real eye-catcher up there along the rolling hills of the countryside. A closer look at the interior wasn't so impressive. The upholstering on the pilot's seat and the double seat just back of it was in sad shape, but we didn't seem to mind. Although we never re-upholstered it, we always lived with the idea that some day we would.

Marvin had his mind set on flying his prize up the Alaska Highway. With that in mind, as soon as summer school was

17

finished, he spent long days piling up his 40 hours he had to have before he would have his private license and be turned loose to fly where he would. On July 28, 1948 he became pilot #1095462.

Fortunately for him, that flight to Alaska never happened. In the 1940's, the Canadians had stiff regulations for American pilots flying through their country. The first prerequisite was a radio that we didn't have.

The J5 had no electrical system, so we had to have a radio built to be operated by a wind-driven generator. The only one we could locate was from a surplus store down in Texas. But when we began to think about mounting it on the underside of the fuselage where it would get the continuous, unobstructed advantage of the wind, and then carrying along a bulky battery to keep it charged, we gave up on the idea entirely. Instead, Marvin made arrangements to ship the plane by rail to Seattle and by boat to Unalakleet, our next year's station in Alaska.

Boyceville, a little town of 500 people, had both a small airport and a railroad going through it. But they weren't in the habit of having airplanes shipped out on flatcars, so our operation kept the whole town entertained for a week. We fumbled around with getting the wings off the plane and by the time we had it accomplished, we had jammed a hole through the fuselage. Neither of us had an idea in the world how we would get it fixed. We crated the wings separately, and three of us carried them, one at a time, through town to the railroad station where the Soo Line had been warned ahead of time and had sent a flatcar up from Minneapolis just for us. By this time, the sidewalks were lined with onlookers, and when we made our last trip down main street pushing the little overgrown orange grasshopper of a fuselage, we had a real audience.

Because we thought possibly no one involved in the routing of our plane would know where Unalakleet was, we put a "Nome, Alaska" tag on it. We didn't see it again until the boat coming up the coast docked at Unalakleet. Then Marvin rode out on the barge, plucked his plane off the ship, and brought it home on the very top of a whole bargeload of cargo. Somewhere along the way the hole in the fuselage had been professionally patched.

Fortunately, we had an aircraft mechanic in Unalakleet. He

not only helped Marvin fasten the wings back in place, but when firecrackers burned three holes through one of the wings on New Year's Eve, he patched them for us, too.

Once the wings had been reunited with the fuselage, the plane had to have an inspection before we dared fly it. That inspection had to be done at Nome, three hundred miles up the coast; and Marvin had a lot of reservations about ferrying it up there. Art Johnson, our local bush pilot who did most of the flying for our public health nurse, didn't have any reservations. So he flew the J5 to Nome for us the last part of August and left it there for whatever repairs the inspector felt necessary in order to have it licensed. A few days later Marvin went to Nome via Alaska Airlines to bring his plane home, and made the longest flight he had made up to that point. Three hours it was from Nome to Unalakleet.

Marvin was appalled at the maintenance bill he was faced with in Nome. He did a little pencil work when he got home and decided that if they actually used all the dope they had charged him for, he would have had thirteen gallons soaked into the fuselage and wings of that little airplane.

"I don't think it could even get off the ground with thirteen gallons of dope on it!" he grumbled.

Flying is more fun if you have a destination. We wanted to put as many hours into the log book as we could, and fortunately, we did have a few places to go. There were numerous thirty minute round trips to Egavik, a deserted village up the coast a few miles, where the reindeer herder kept his herd. From the looks of his log book, Marvin kept the herd well-supervised that fall. Shaktoolik was a nice village with a questionable landing strip and a family we enjoyed visiting on weekends. Dick and Nellie Collard were the teachers. They always made us welcome, and our Cyndie played well with their four little boys.

We kept the plane tied down just outside the fence around the teacherage, and had it weighted down with drums of oil. I remember the night with an unusually high wind ripping, when one of our neighbors came running in all out of breath.

"Warbelow! Your plane is blowing away!"

"It can't be blowing away. I've got it tied down to three drums of oil."

"But it is! It is!"

Sure enough. The plane with its three barrels of fuel was sliding all over the back yard.

It was shortly after that when Marvin came home late one night and landed on the ocean ice just in front of the village. Because it was near dark, we considered leaving the plane down there until morning. But we changed our minds, and before bedtime, pushed it up onto shore and into its parking place. The next morning we discovered an offshore wind had taken out the ice and we had nothing but open water for a half mile.

On the thirteenth of October, Marvin made a flight down the coast to St. Michael to pick up some books from the Paul Ivanoff's, who were teaching there. The St. Michael landing strip at that time was just the ocean beach at low tide, so it was usually littered with driftwood debris and was filled with swales left in the sand by pounding waves. Marvin managed to get down all right, but on take-off his wooden prop hit a high spot between two swales and the end broke off. Paul located a hacksaw and together they squared off the shattered end of the prop, then sawed off the other one to match it. Late that night our little J5 came putt-putting home sounding as though the engine was ready to shake to pieces.

Little disasters followed us right up until the day the J5 left for its new home. We were transferring from Unalakleet to Selawik, right up on the Arctic Circle, during the holiday season. So three days after New Year's, Marvin had the plane loaded with household goods and gear, intending to make the flight to Selawik alone. Cyndie, her new baby brother Ron, and I were to follow later. Daylight was a scarce item, so it was still dark when Marvin, well-bundled in parka and mukluks, bid us all good-bye and left the house.

Selawik was a two-hour flight away, and except for a few miles of flatland circling Norton Sound, the entire route was mountainous all the way to the broad Selawik valley to the northeast.

Right after take-off, Marvin put all 85 horses to work in order to gain altitude before he reached the hills, but the plane didn't seem to be responding. In a matter of minutes, he had run out of flat country, and in no way could he clear the hills. He made a couple of big circles, trying to gain altitude, but was still plugging along at about 400 feet. Baffled, he turned around and came back to the village. It was then he discovered that the entire back end of the fuselage was packed full of snow. By the time he had cleaned it out, he had run out of daylight, so tied down and came home for the night.

The morning of January 5, 1950 he was up long before daylight to get his fire-potting done. With a fresh load of fuel, he started out once again. This time he didn't come back, but he didn't get very far either. Ceilings were low and visibility over the mountains bad, so he hung close to the Sound, crossed the open water of Norton Bay, and stopped for the night at Koyuk.

Three days later the Koyuk teachers were still hosting him. But the following morning things looked a little better, so he made his next hop. The Buckland River was the only real landmark, about halfway between Koyuk and Selawik to the north. But he couldn't get far enough inland to find the Buckland. Weather kept squeezing him to the west, and this time he spent the night with the missionaries at Candle, just to the south of Kotzebue Sound.

It should have been a simple flight from Candle to Selawik if he fringed the Sound and Selawik Lake, but somehow he missed his target. Once he broke into the Selawik Valley, all his landmarks suddenly disappeared. He had never seen the valley before; and nothing but miles of flat, swampy terrain, almost more water than land, stretched as far as he could see. The valley was an endless tangle of rivulets, potholes, and swamps. On a clear day, one could see the range of hills 80 miles to the north that separates the Selawik and Kobuk Valleys.

Aiming at what he thought would eventually become the Selawik River, he explored first one and then another wrong lead until, with his fuel tank running low and daylight again fading, he decided he would have to set down for the night. But he turned around first to take one more look down the ribbon of frozen ice he had been following, and there ahead of him was a mass of tiny lights, crowded together, and twinkling dimly up from

21

Selawik.

That night he logged his 65th hour.

CHAPTER III

The airplane was a real novelty at Selawik. Flying teachers were a scarcity, and the villagers loved having that big bird tied down on the river below the bank in front of the school.

Early in February, Marvin made a flight to Kotzebue to pick up some parcels we had mailed from Unalakleet. He had strong head winds on the way home, but he didn't realize the seriousness of his situation until he discovered that he couldn't get ahead of a dog team traveling across Selawik Lake. Once again darkness caught up with him. He landed on the lake and anchored the plane as best he could. Then he dug a tunnel into the side of a snowdrift, curled up inside it, and stayed there until morning.

By mid-February days were lengthening enough for a few nice hours of sunlight to pour down on us. Marvin made the most of it. Few of our school children had ever been in a plane. So often on a nice noon hour or after school, he hand-propped the J5, loaded two youngsters in the back seat, and took them up for a few circles around the village. By late March every kid in school who wanted one, had had a ride.

The adults got in on a few trips, too. Shee-fishing was the popular early spring sport, and by March the fish were biting in Selawik Lake. Johnny Foster, who had struck up quite a friendship with Marvin, convinced him they should fly the ten miles down to the lake some weekend and do a bit of fishing.

That proved to be a weekend Marvin might better have just stayed in bed. Saturday morning, he and Johnny gathered up their fishing gear and took off. They landed near one end of the lake, but the bulk of the village was already down at the opposite end, settled in at their fishing holes. The fellows didn't want to walk far, so decided they would taxi down instead. This was fine until they hit a frozen drift, and broke the left landing gear. They had to hook a ride home with one of the dog teams, and that night the men in the village went into conference to decide how to get the plane back home.

Next morning, Marvin and three men with teams went back to the lake with an empty sled. With the sled lashed under the broken ski and the three teams strung out in a single line, they pulled the plane upriver those ten miles. But when they got within a mile or so of home, several others mushed out to meet them, tied their own teams, one in front of the other, to the already long line of dogs, and came into Main Street with that little blob of orange behind thirty-five dogs.

That put an end to the fun for the rest of the winter. We didn't know where or how to get a replacement gear, so my brother-in-law started looking for one back in Wisconsin. With mail service once a month, nothing was happening very fast.

The one-legged bird was still sitting there on the ice a few weeks later when Bert Beltz heard about it. He talked another Kotzebue pilot into flying him up to Selawik one morning, looked over the situation, and offered us $500 for the plane where it was, as it was. With no alternative in mind, we took his offer. But when he came back a few days later with a piece of plywood, toggled up the ski, and took off with no problem at all, we were deflated to say the least.

CHAPTER IV

The summer of 1950 we were back in Wisconsin again. My uncle, who was working at Ladd Field in Fairbanks for the summer, let us drive his little Willys Knight four-cylinder car on our first trip ever down the Alaska Highway.

We started looking hard for another airplane. The doctor who had delivered Cyndie, had a nice little Cessna 140 he wanted to sell. Marvin, wanting to try something besides another Piper, was interested.

The day we went to look at it, I was astounded. "Marvin, this plane is like new! I thought we were thinking about something used. The uphostering isn't even ripped. We just can't afford something like this."

"You can have anything in this world you want if you're willing to work hard enough for it," Marvin stated gravely. "Someday, we're going to have a brand new plane."

We didn't buy the 140. Doc wanted $1500 for it and wouldn't be talked down. So we did some more shopping around, and finally located another 140 in equally good condition up at Siren, a hundred miles north, for a thousand dollars. The 140's had a bad habit of nosing over, so extensions on the front landing gear were common modifications. This plane had the extensions.

The fellow we bought it from owned a bar uptown. Marvin didn't mention the fact to him that he had already come close to buying a Cessna 140, had flown the doctor's plane, and knew what he wanted. They went up for a 15-minute hop; and when they taxied back to their parking spot, Marvin said, "Well, should we go uptown and close the deal."

I'm sure the fellow had thought he was just angling a free ride. He took a quick glance at Marvin's faded blue jeans and chambray shirt left over from his Maritime Service days, and shook his head.

"I want cash. You don't have a thousand dollars on you!"

Marvin pulled a roll of ten one-hundred dollar bills out of his pocket and strung them out like a hand of cards. They went uptown and closed the deal.

Once again Marvin made plans to fly a plane up the Alaska Highway, and again his plans fell through. I was supposed to drive the car north with the two small children while he flew. But I backed out, probably because we got very little support from our families on such a trip. The Alaska Highway in 1950, was still nothing much better than a cow trail in some spots.

We went back to Boyceville to think the matter over. But we didn't have long to think. The next day Harvey Engen from the Siren area, appeared at the farmhouse door and asked for Marvin. When he found out we had gone to the nearby town of Menomonie and were driving a car with an Alaska license, he drove up and down every street in town until he found us. Harvey had just received his commercial pilot's license, made a cross-country flight to Florida, and wanted to fly the 140 to Fairbanks for us.

Hull insurance for the trip was prohibitive and Marvin wasn't at all sold on the idea of turning his plane over to a stranger. But Harvey was one of the most determined young fellows we had ever seen. A month later, when we drove into the airport at Weeks Field in Fairbanks, our little red and silver Cessna was sitting there waiting for us. We took Harvey out for spaghetti dinner at the old Model Cafe on Second Avenue that night, and the next day put him on a plane back to Wisconsin.

That was the first of many long flights for Harvey. He never gave up on his dream of becoming an Air Transport Rated pilot. It took him a few years to get there, but he flew co-pilot and finally Captain for Northwest Airlines for many years, and we always kept in touch.

CHAPTER V

The 140 stayed with us for the next two years at Selawik. For a plane as inadequate as it was, it hung in there better than we had expected it to. Marvin built a little jump seat in back of the double seat in front. With Cyndie on that and Ron in my lap, we made short trips to the surrounding villages, and a few flights back to Unalakleet. When one of my teeth needed filling, we left the children with the baby sitter and flew to Nome for a dental appointment. The dentist, known well in Western Alaska as "the flying dentist" because he had his own plane and flew out to the villages with his portable dental equipment, was interested in our trip.

"Do you fly around Selawik Lake or go across it?" he asked.

"We go straight across it," Marvin told him.

"You're foolish. *Very* foolish! That's too much water to be crossing on wheels."

We never saw him again. He was a handsome and successful young man, a good dentist, and popular with everyone. But shortly after our visit to him he committed suicide and no one ever seemed to know why.

By May, the river ice was getting mushy, and our winter landing strip wasn't going to last much longer. Johnny Beltz came in one day from Kotzebue with his little yellow Piper J3. Johnny was a self-made pilot. A crippling childhood disease had left him with a badly deformed back, and Johnny had the idea that because of this, he would never be able to pass a physical for his pilot's license. So he learned to fly this way or that, bought himself a plane, and spent years avoiding the CAA inspectors.

On this particular day, Johnny was getting ready to leave for his trip back to Kotzebue just as Marvin was on the radio with the ACS (Alaska Communications System) for his nightly schedule. The voice at the other end of the wire said, most casually, "Does Johnny Beltz happen to be there?"

When Marvin assured him that yes, Johnny was there, the voice said, "You might mention to him that the CAA inspector is in town."

Marvin whirled around in his chair and called to me, "Stop Johnny, quick!"

Ben Foxglove was in the shop cleaning up after his crafts class, so I ran to relay the message to him. At the same time I glanced out the window to see Johnny with his prop going, and already climbing into his seat.

Ben went plowing down the hill, waving wildly at Johnny. He stopped him just in time. I watched them as they exchanged a few words. Then Johnny cut the motor, the prop slowed to a standstill, and the two fellows tied the plane down again. Johnny had suddenly decided to spend the night in Selawik.

The next afternoon at radio schedule time, Johnny was sitting in the office beside Marvin. The voice from Kotzebue said, and again in a very low key, "Is Johnny around there yet?"

"Yes, I think he must be. I see his plane is still sitting down here on the river."

"You might mention to him that the CAA inspector left this morning."

So Johnny went sliding down the river bank, warmed up his J3, and left for Kotzebue.

It was two or three years later when the CAA inspectors finally convinced him that he'd have no trouble passing a physical. And at long last Johnny became legal.

We first knew of Tommy Richards when he was a young pilot for Wien Airlines flying the mail runs out of Kotzebue to Selawik, and then over into the Kobuk Valley all the way up the river to Noorvik, Kiana, Shungnak, and Kobuk. Tommy was a handsome

Eskimo man, and one of the most idolized bush pilots in the area. He flew good weather and bad weather, and never lost his cool.

I remember especially, the day Tommy stopped off in Selawik with his load of mail and visited with Marvin long enough to mention the fact that the float plane he was flying had just come back from an annual inspection in Fairbanks. The Selawik airstrip was hardly fit for a human to land on during the summer months, so all the commercial pilots came in only on floats.

With his small bag of outgoing mail slung into the back seat, Tommy took off toward Shungnak, but within fifteen minutes he was back again. The sound of his motor in the distance, growing louder instead of fading away, alerted everyone in the village.

Once Tommy was within sight, we could see the fabric on one side of the plane flapping in the wind, and the size of the flap grew larger every instant. His floats touched down on the river, and by this time the ribs of the fuselage were showing almost to the tail.

Marvin jumped into his boat, snapped the pull cord of the motor, and was at the plane before Tommy had come to a complete stop. The wind had caught a loose corner of the fabric at the edge of his windshield and peeled it back like a banana, but Tommy crawled carefully down onto the float and into the boat with complete poise, just as though this was an everyday occurance.

The two men rummaged around in our shop and found enough patching material in our plane supplies to put the skin back together. Then, in his own self-confident, quiet way, Tommy crawled back into his plane and took off, but not toward Kotzebue as we had expected him to. He nosed up the canyon toward Shungnak, a hundred miles away, to go on with his mail run.

We had a four-day storm in January of 1952 such as we had never seen before. Winds registered to over 100 knots an hour in Kotzebue, and there was just no let-up.

The 140 was tied down to weights frozen into the river ice in front of the school. But even from our spot at the top of the bank not more than 200 feet away, we couldn't see it because of blowing snow and blizzard conditions. The wind kept shifting, and by the end of the fourth day had made a complete 360 degree turn. Because it was essential that we keep the plane nosed into the wind, Marvin had to make trips down to the plane every few hours and soon resorted to tying it to oil drums that could be shifted as the wind shifted.

On one of those first trips back home, he lost his bearings and finally bumped into a house two cabins down the path from us. After that experience, we tied a long rope to the doorknob, and Marvin dragged it down the hill with him to help him find his way back.

But all the watching and tying and moving of the plane didn't do much good. When the storm finally wore itself out and we could see the results, not only did we have house roofs, loose oil drums, sleds, and debris scattered all over the village, but one of our plane wings was twisted like a piece of taffy.

Marvin and Ray Skin, the school janitor, took matters in hand. Right after breakup, they lashed the broken wing onto Ray's 30-foot river boat and made a trip across Kobuk Lake to Kotzebue with it. While Ray caught up on his visiting in town, Marvin and Bill Laws, an aircraft mechanic, spent a week rebuilding the wing.

The trip back across the lake was a rough one, and at times the men thought they were going to capsize, or at least lose the wing. But neither of these things really happened, and they made it back to the village during the night. Tired and cold, they tied the boat and crawled into bed.

Next morning before we could get the wing unloaded, a plane came in from Kotzebue with some traveling government personnel on board. We put on the coffee pot, and while we were sitting around the kitchen table chatting, we suddenly realized a strong wind had come up. Marvin thought of the boat with the wing on it, jumped up and went dashing out the office door. The wing was already bouncing up and down on the boat. It took all four of the men who had been at the table to hold it down while Marvin got it untied. By that time he already had a dent along the leading edge.

By the spring of 1952, we had made up our minds that the 140 just wasn't for us any more. Although the front leg extensions had probably saved us from disaster more than once, the plane was obviously under-powered. So we began to noise it around the country that we wanted to sell, as we planned to go state-side again that summer and wanted to bring back a bigger plane. Nelson Walker was in one day from Kotzebue with his Cub, and stopped by for coffee.

"How much are you asking for the plane?" he asked.

"I want $1600," Marvin told him.

"I don't think you can get that much for it," Nelson decided.

"Well, *I'll* sell it for $1400 if we have to," I declared. "I want to get rid of that thing before it kills us."

We had no takers, and as May slipped by and the plane still sat out on the river, we decided we would have to get it off the ice before it broke through or floated down to Kotzebue with the ice pack. So finally, in desperation, we made up our minds to fly it to Fairbanks, tie it down for the summer, and hope to get a buyer there.

The nights stayed warm and there was no crust of frozen snow on the river for an early morning take-off with four of us in the plane. But on the slough at the other side of the village, conditions were a little better. Marvin and Ray Skin marked off a thousand feet of what they considered the safest spot for a take-off. A thousand feet was all they could get.

Early on the morning of June 2, Ray helped us carry the kids and our limited gear across the mush of the river and the strip of land that separated the river from the slough. We settled into the plane, Marvin took off his hip boots and handed them to Ray to take back to the school; and on a wing and a prayer, believe me, we started down the short strip of honeycombed ice with its layer of soft snow. For some reason we made it. The plane barely lifted just as we crossed the last inch of that thousand feet, and we were on our way.

In all his flying in the arctic, Marvin never went a straight line to Fairbanks. We routed ourselves through Unalakleet and finally up the Yukon River to Tanana. At breakup time the Yukon can be a mile wide in spots, and the whole country was flooded. Trees along the way were half submerged in water. If we had had to set

31

down, there was no way in the world we could have found a spot.

Our plans were to stay overnight at Tanana with the Walt Hart family who were there with the CAA, and go on to Fairbanks in the morning. But we had barely gotten settled in when Walt called Marvin from the control room to tell him he had a wire from Harold Lei in Kotzebue. The wire read, "If you will bring that plane back to Kotzebue, I'll give you $1500 for it."

How we wished that we had been one day later or that Harold had been a day earlier! But we couldn't afford to pass up the sale. So the next morning Marvin fired up, turned the nose to the west, and started on that long trip back to Kotzebue.

Harold was there waiting for Marvin with $1500 in hand.

"How did you know I would sell the plane for $1500?" Marvin asked him.

"Nelson Walker told me."

Nelson had evidently struck a happy medium and come up with a price satisfactory to everyone.

Donald Ferguson was flying a scheduled run from Kotzebue to Fairbanks those days in a beautiful plush Beechcraft Bonanza his dad had given him. So the next day, here came Donald and Marvin enroute to Fairbanks, stopping by Tanana to pick up the rest of us. That was my first and last ride in a V-tail Bonanza, and I was amused to see that 20-year old Donald, so small he had to sit on a cushion in order to reach the pedals, sitting at the controls of this beautiful plane.

CHAPTER VI

We had outgrown a J5 and we had outgrown a 140. The next logical step up was to a Cessna 170. The 170 was a popular plane with a lot more advantages than disadvantages. It had four ample seats, had enough power to carry four passengers and their gear, was economical to operate, and cruised at 140 knots. We still weren't at that station in life where Marvin could have the brand new plane he dreamed about, so we went through the pages of "Trade-A-Plane" in search of what we wanted. Cessna 170's were plentiful and there always seemed to be several for sale. The going price then and for several years to come, was $3500. We found what we thought we wanted down in Des Moines.

We had bought a car that summer to use while we were in Wisconsin, but had no use for it in Alaska, so when Marvin phoned the air service in Des Moines, they agreed that if we bought the plane, they would take the car on a trade-in.

When we got to Des Moines, the plane was on a charter to Chicago and wasn't going to be back for a couple of days. Des Moines was full of polio and since we had the children with us, we didn't want to stay over. So we decided that we would pick the plane up in LaCrosse, Wisconsin, where my brother lived. The air service radioed their pilot to drop the plane off in LaCrosse and drive on to Des Moines in the car.

The deal was closed. No money changed hands, but we were to pay cash to the pilot when we met him in LaCrosse. It was pouring rain that day, and when we got ready to leave, Marvin asked, "Aren't you going to come out and take a look at the car?"

"No," came the reply. "I don't want to get wet. If you can take the plane sight unseen, I guess I can take the car the same way."

We were waiting at the LaCrosse airport when our silver plane with a graceful red stripe along each side taxied in and stopped. We walked up to it, and the closer we got, the bigger it looked.

"It's sure big, isn't it!" Marvin whispered.

Trying to act casual and confident and experienced, he shook hands with the pilot, and gave a couple of finger snaps to the rag wing to get a feel for its airworthiness. We stood side by side at the left wingtip while he exchanged a few routine remarks with the pilot. Then he began slowly walking around the plane, first to the prop, then the right wing tip, and finally to the tail. He slid his hands over the tail pieces and up the back of the fuselage a bit, scrutinizing every inch carefully.

"Looks like a few dents here in the end of the fuselage," he remarked. The pilot was silent.

Marvin finally arrived at the first wing tip where we stood waiting for him.

"How much is your boss going to let you knock off on this?" he asked.

With a sigh of boredom and a lift of an eyebrow, the fellow said, "A hundred fifty. No more."

"That suits me fine. Let's go into the office here and get the deal settled."

Marvin had his money in hand and the pilot had the paperwork, so within a few minutes the pilot was on his way to Des Moines and we stood at the wing tip while Marvin made a second trip around the plane, and as he circled it I could see this strange look on his face becoming more evident with every step. Finally he completed his circle.

"Lou," he admitted, "I don't think I can fly this thing!"

I fairly gasped. "You mean we're heading for the Arctic Circle tomorrow morning with two little kids — and *you* can't fly the airplane!"

Marvin bit his lip a bit and thought it over. "I think," he said, "I'd better get an instructor to go up with me for a few landings."

There was an instructor on hand at the field, so they took the plane up for about fifteen minutes while Marvin shot some landings and got the feel of this newest of his toys.

"How much time have you had in a 170?" he asked, once they were airborne.

"I've never been in a 170 before," came the reply.

That plane felt like a palace to us. For the first time we had a seat apiece, and the kids could be properly belted into the two seats behind us.

My brother and his wife took us to the airport the next morning and saw us off. It was July 21 and that was our mother's birthday. That, I thought, must be a good omen. And indeed it was, for a few days at least.

We had beautiful weather and good flying all across the country to Montana and up past Edmonton. But as we got into the mountains, winds became a real problem. I think the only thing that kept us right side up at all was the fact that we carried ten gallons of extra fuel with us all the way. Airfields were a long ways apart, and most of the planes that made that trip were small ones with a limited range. The Canadians had cleared out emergency landing strips along the highway just in case a plane had to stop to refuel. And one of their regulations was that you never let the Alaska Highway out of your sight. You were allowed no shortcuts.

Although we were well-equipped with emergency food, an axe, sleeping bags, and everything we thought we would need in case of a forced landing, it didn't meet Canadian regulations. At Edmonton the officials wouldn't let us leave until we had purchased one of their thirty dollar ready-made emergency kits all sealed up in a yellow metal case. We didn't have to use it, so Marvin carried it around in the plane with him for another year or so, thinking he had some good emergency gear with him. Finally one day we got curious, so broke the seal and opened it up, only to find about all there was in it was oatmeal.

The trip was rough on Marvin and me, but rougher on the

children. Once in the air, they'd get bored with just sitting for hours, so would unbuckle their seat belts, play around a bit, and usually end up all over the floor in a wrestling match. Whenever we got within a few miles of our next stop, Marvin would yell back at them, "Fasten your seat belts!"

Cyndie always obediently climbed back into her seat and clicked her belt shut. But Ron, not three years old yet, was a doubter. Invariably he would stand on tiptoe, clutch the bottom edge of the window, peer out, and say, "I don't tee no airtip." Just as invariably, Marvin would cut the power, and we could hear Ron scrambling for his seat.

Meals were a big problem all along the way. We always managed a good breakfast every morning, but that was usually the last meal we got until we stopped at night. There was never any place at the airports to buy food, and we didn't want to take the precious time to go uptown. The kids didn't survive very well on packaged crackers and dried fruit.

There was a construction camp at the Grande Prairie airport, and the fellow who gassed the plane said I might find something to eat at the company mess hall. The cook was sleeping when I walked in, and a young fellow was washing dishes. When I asked him if we could buy a meal, he nodded his head toward the refrigerator.

"Help yourself," he said.

I felt a little strange, but I certainly didn't turn down his offer. Into that refrigerator I dived. I hauled out a loaf of bread and three platters of half-eaten pork and beef roasts, all a little dried around the edges. By the time Marvin got his gas paid for and arrived at the kitchen, I had four big sandwiches made up. We sat on the edge of the table while we gobbled them down, finished off with some wedges of pumpkin pie, tipped the boy a couple of dollars, and were on our way.

Fort Nelson didn't make much of a splash on the map in the early fifties. At best you might call it an outpost on the Alaska Highway. We paid a dollar a gallon for gas pumped from fifty gallon drums and poured into our tanks with jeep cans.

The only hotel in town was built of old army surplus quonset huts, musty smelling and dark. The town got its power from the army base eight miles away. So when the army had mechanical problems and cut the power off for several hours that night, we were not only without light, but water. The creamed corn we had for dinner had been made with sour milk, and no one could eat it. But they must have used up that left-over milk the next morning, because the pancakes were perfect.

Whitehorse was a disaster. By the time we got there we had plowed through three days of rain, fog, and turbulent winds. Marvin was tired and uptight. He still hadn't figured out how to manage the airplane. As he said some years later in reminiscing, "I didn't fly that plane up the highway. *It* flew *me*!"

The Whitehorse airport is at the top of a hill high above town. From the air we could see two runways, side by side, and the highway at right angles to the strip at one end. There was a sheer drop-off of several hundred feet at the other end.

Marvin radioed in his position and asked for permission to land. We were just coming into our pattern when the voice from the tower said, "Land right."

Marvin went to pieces. He had never heard of making a right-hand pattern; but after all, this was Canada, and maybe that was the way they did it here. He didn't have time to consider the fact that he had been in Canada for several days now and nowhere had he been told to "land right."

He made a 180 degree turn, and proceeded to circle the field in a right hand pattern. It was enough to shake even a seasoned pilot, and that he wasn't. He made a poor landing and the plane bounced thirty feet into the air and hit the runway. Just at that moment Marvin saw a sign along the edge of the strip indicating that we were on the military strip and not the civilian. Completely out of control, the plane made another thirty foot leap into the air, and then a third one. We had leap-frogged the entire length of the landing strip and that cliff was just ahead of us. In desperation he nosed the plane up and we took off again. By this time he realized that the order to "land right" meant to land on the right runway and not the left one. He made a conventional left-hand pattern and brought the plane down on the civilian strip where we should have been in the first place.

Three fellows stood at the door of the control room watching the performance. "What on earth were you trying to do?" one of them asked.

"Well, I didn't know what the heck you meant by 'land right'!" Marvin began defensively.

But before he could say more, the three men broke into laughs. "You're not the first one who has landed on the wrong strip," one of them assured him. "We get a show like this every once in a while."

It poured rain in Whitehouse. Our room at the hotel had no heat in it; and since our clothes and especially our shoes were soaked, we shivered miserably there for a day and a half. Fortunately, the little cafe where we ate was warm and friendly, and we managed to eat a lot of long drawn-out meals.

It was still raining when we finally got off again the next afternoon. We plowed through the soup until we got a few minutes past Delta. Sheets of rain completely blinded us and we finally had to turn back. There wasn't a hotel or motel in Delta at the time, so the Army put us up at Fort Greely where we sat for two more days before we could get in the air again. We tried to stay in our room and be as low-key as possible for fear of getting evicted, but with two small children, that wasn't easy to do. The GI's were delighted to have them on base, and made them the center of attraction in the mess hall.

We went without dinner our first night, not knowing for sure whether we would be allowed to eat there or not. But the next morning we were in the mess hall for breakfast. The fellows dishing up food at the counter piled Ron's plate high, and kept adding more food as long as he nodded his head. He not only sat down to a plateful of three fried eggs, potatoes, bacon, toast, a fresh tomato, and a chunk of cantaloupe, plus two glasses of milk, but he ate it all. I shuddered in shame. The boys probably thought we hadn't fed the kids in days, and that was just about the truth.

Two weeks after we left LaCrosse, we finally came within sight of Selawik. We circled the stretch of tundra that was the only summer strip the village had, and it was obvious that only one plane had landed there all the two months we were gone. The grass was two to three feet tall, and down the center of it was one lone trail, chopped through by someone's propeller blades. But while we were circling and debating, half the populace in the village jumped into boats and made their way to the field. In a matter of minutes, twenty or thirty of them were lined up along both edges of the strip wildly waving us in.

"I can't see what's underneath that grass, and I don't trust those fellows as far as I can see them," Marvin mumbled. "They'd wave anybody in no matter what the field is like, just so they can see what you're there for."

He was right. After twenty minutes of circling, he sat down. The plane came to a dead stop and sank into six inches of mud. We didn't nose over, but I don't know why.

Nor did the plane move off the field on its own power. We had to bring big 2 x 6's over from the school to put under the wheels and pry them out of the mud. A dozen willing hands pushed our stranded 170 off the field to dry land, and there it sat until the end of August when nights got chilly enough to put a frozen crust on the tundra.

CHAPTER VII

Election day in November of 1952 began a series of plane catastrophes in the Kotzebue area that we thought would never end. By sheer luck we hadn't been able to get any skis yet, so at least we were forced to stay on the ground.

John Cross, flying the mail for Wiens, started up the Kobuk. He made it to Noorvik and Kiana, but about halfway between Kiana and Shungnak ran into bad weather and had to set down at Hunt River. He radioed in to Kotzebue, but Wiens didn't have anything on skis yet, so Nelson Walker with his Cub, started out to rescue him. Weather had been unusually good that morning, and no one realized that a sudden storm was right at the back door. All the planes in Kotzebue were out that morning, and everyone got caught short. Nelson, with a pair of skis for John's plane with him, didn't get much above Kiana when the weather closed in so bad he had to find a spot to land until the snow let up a little. By the time he was able to get off again and make Hunt River, it was dark; so both he and John were stuck for another night. The next morning they got the skis on John's plane and made it back to Kotzebue.

That same morning a plane from the radar station up at Cape Lisbourne above Point Hope tried to reach Kotzebue with four passengers aboard. They got into a whiteout situation, flew into the ice, and totalled the plane, although no one was seriously hurt. The radio was still operable, so the pilot radioed into Kotzebue; and a DC3 just getting ready to take off for Nome, went out on instruments to locate them. Even at 250 feet, they still couldn't

41

see the crash; but the two pilots were keeping in contact through the CAA station in Kotzebue, and the pilot on the ground could direct the rescue plane by the sound of his motor. For some reason, the two radios couldn't communicate directly with one another.

Once the DC3 had the location, it just circled until Tommy Richards and Billy Levi could get out there in their two single engine planes to land and pick up the five people stranded on the ice. But things got sticky before they finally accomplished it. Although the CAA kept in contact with the DC3, once Billy and Tommy got that far out of Kotzebue and flying at such low altitudes, the CAA lost contact with both of them. There was no way to tell them that the DC3 was right down there on the deck at their own level and all three flying in close quarters. All of us there in the arctic with our radios on, listening to the whole scenario were pacing the floor and biting fingernails until the rescue was completed and all three planes were safely back in Kotzebue. Dr. Rabeau at the Alaska Native Health Service hospital patched up all the bruises on the crash victims, and life in the arctic settled back to normal for a short time.

We had hardly cooled off from all this when the National Guard started its big airlift of Guardsmen from all over the Territory for a rally at Anchorage. Bush pilots were to pick up the men from their villages and fly them to places like Kotzebue, Nome, Barrow, and Unalakleet where there were strips along enough for the National Guard's own planes to land and take them on into Anchorage. Bush pilots in the arctic were running hungry those days, and it became a real race to see who could get there first. Those last three days before the deadline, weather turned foul; but pilots were willing to do anything to get an extra fare, so they kept on flying. That's when their trouble began.

We heard one man take off from Kotzebue one of those mornings and figured he would be at Selawik in forty-five minutes, so I put the coffee pot on. But the man never arrived. The last CAA heard from him, he was over Kobuk Lake and said weather was closing in, and then there was nothing from him for two hours. By the time he was fifteen minutes overdue on his return trip, they began calling him, and eventually got a response. He claimed he had been flying around those two hours looking for a hole, but the man didn't have that kind of gas in his tanks, so we all assumed there was a part of the story he never told.

That same day a small bush outfit sent a 170 just like ours up to Wainwright to pick up three Guardsmen and take them on up to Barrow. Just as they were letting down for a landing at the Barrow strip, they crashed into the ocean and all four were killed.

The next afternoon, another man made a last minute run up to Shungnak to get the last of the men out of there. But on the way back, something went wrong; and he had to make a forced landing at Hunt River. A friend went right up that same evening, ferried part of his load into Kiana, and then went back to pick up the rest of them. We never heard what went wrong with the first plane, but a week later it still wasn't in the air.

While all this was happening, a CAA mechanic from Galena started out in his Stinson for Nenana, and disappeared. He had contacted the Tanana CAA once, but they couldn't locate him. For the next three days, there were twenty planes from the Fairbanks area including the Army, out searching for him, but with no luck. Then six days later, he showed up, on foot, on the bank of the Yukon about twenty miles from Tanana. He had run out of gas, crash-landed, and walked out. A few days later he wrote Tundra Topics, a Fairbanks radio program, and said he had a word of advice to pass along to other pilots. With two more gallons of gas, he could have made it into an airfield, and he recalled when he started out from Galena that morning, he had a gas tank that could have held five more gallons.

Our last big crisis took place up at the Cape Lisbourne communications site. The towers there were built at the top of some rugged mountains, and they had to transport men and equipment up with a tramway. One afternoon the cable broke with ten men in the car. They crashed down the mountain, and three of them were seriously injured. A message went out to the army post in Anchorage, and the Tenth Rescue team started out immediately with a doctor aboard. They had a trip of several hundred miles ahead of them, so it was seven-thirty that night before they reached Lisbourne. Once again, all of us in the arctic were monitoring their trip, minute by minute, all afternoon and evening.

The Lisbourne field wasn't lighted, and it was a tricky place to get in to. It was basically just a 3600 foot strip of beach with the ocean on one side and thousand foot cliffs on the other. The pilots had never been up there before, so all along the way, CAA stations were monitoring them and keeping them posted on weather ahead. The station at Koztebue was even contacting all the local bush pilots to give the rescue plane a description of the field he would be landing on. This was arctic cooperation at its best — just another reason for our being proud of our neighbors who peopled this barren and unrelenting country. Everyone who could do anything at all to aid the rescue was doing it to his utmost.

The fellows up at Lisbourne stationed a truck at each of the four corners of the strip with lights on, and lined both sides of the field with lanterns mounted on oil drums. Every available lantern in the village was recruited.

With a 500 foot ceiling, the pilot had to fly instruments until he was ready to let down at Lisbourne. He came in close enough so those on the ground could hear his motors, then he turned out over the ocean, and it was five minutes before they heard him again and he finally landed. There was dead silence on all the airways while everyone waited, hoping, and that was a lo-o-n-g five minutes for all of us.

In the meantime, they were having a lot of difficulty getting the injured men down off the mountain. Weasel trails were blocked with snow, and there was such a glare of ice they couldn't get the snowplow through to make a trail. At least one of the men was a stretcher case, and this added to their difficulties. But eventually they got the victims down to level ground, and that doctor was a welcome sight.

The winter of 1952-53 was a miserable one for me. Our third baby was due in May, and I was being beset with cravings for all sorts of food we didn't have. Donald Ferguson was making scheduled flights into Fairbanks with the Bonanza, so Marvin radioed down to him to bring back a dozen apples for us on his next flight.

The morning after his next return from Fairbanks, we flew down to Kotzbue to pick up my fruit. Archie Ferguson had built a nice apartment for his family upstairs above his store, all finished off in

Philippine mahogany. We walked upstairs, knocked on the door, and heard Archie in the distance yell for us to come in. The kitchen table was piled with boxes and packages obviously unloaded there in a hurry, but at a glance we didn't see anything that looked like a sack of apples.

"Archie," Marvin called into the living room, "did Donald bring us any apples from Fairbanks yesterday?"

"Oh, was them your apples?" cackled the voice from the next room. "Gee, they was good!"

The truth of the matter was, Archie had gotten away with only two of my pieces of fruit. I still had ten huge Delicious apples left to take home with us.

Dick and Billie Taylor, the school teachers at Kiana, had never been to Nome. So we made plans for Dick to go with us when Marvin took me down to the hospital, and Billie would have her trip when he came to pick me up.

We waited as long as we dared, but the river ice was getting soft, and with a fluke of weather we could very well be without an airstrip, so on April 27, Marvin flew Cyndie and Ron over to Kiana to stay with Billie, and brought Dick back with him. I was all ready to go when they arrived at Selawik, and we had a beautiful trip to Nome. That was big city stuff to all of us. Main Street, a federal building, board sidewalks, and the Polaris Hotel. We booked in at the Polaris and went out to a real restaurant for dinner. The fellows would like to have stayed over another day, but their better judgement told them they should be on their way. We took a cab and I went out to the airfield with them to see them off, but let the cab leave because I wanted to walk back to town. Bert Beltz was wandering around out there like a lost soul, so he walked back with me and brought me up to date on the fate of our little J5.

We had heard stories over the past couple of years of Bert's various crack-ups with the plane, but he always managed to get it back in the air again. Then he moved it from Kotzebue to Nome, and there a couple of times, some of his acquaintances had helped themselves to it, and even done some damage to it in one instance. Finally someone had crash-landed it out on the tundra and there it stayed. There wasn't enough left to salvage.

"This time they'll either pay for it or I'm suing for a thousand dollars!" Bert assured me emphatically. But Bert was an easygoing sort, and I doubt he ever pursued the matter.

I hadn't seen a doctor in nine months, so as soon as Bert and I parted ways I went directly up to Dr. Langsom's office. I was still sitting in the waiting room when another patient remarked to anyone who might be interested, "Did you know Billy Levi was killed this morning?" Billy Levi was one of our friends back home.

I thought I would die on the spot. "My God!" I gasped, "What happened?"

Billy had gone out to Shishmareff that morning to pick up a girl from the village and take her back to Kotzebue. Visibility was almost zero. He flew into the ice and killed both of them. His wristwatch stopped on impact, and registered the exact instant of the crash.

Billy's story was a tragic one. He had landed twice after his take-off from Shishmareff before his fatal crash, but each time had attempted to go on. He must have had a feeling he might not make it because in each instance he had taken the time to log the landings.

Why did he do it? Why did he take such a risk? The only answer anyone could come up with was the fact that Billy had been drafted into the Army and was supposed to be in Kotzebue that afternoon to meet the plane that would be picking up the draftees.

Dr. Langsom was perturbed with me. My blood pressure was way up, and although I insisted Marvin had been taking it regularly all winter and there had been nothing wrong with it, he put me on an austere diet. He just wouldn't believe Billy Levi's death had anything to do with it.

I didn't have much of a stay in Nome. Six days after I arrived, our new son Charlie was born. I got back from the delivery room at 11:30, just in time to eat the chicken and ice cream Sunday dinner. A few minutes later, Dr. Langsom appeared.

"When do you want to go home?" he asked.

"Go home! Migosh, I just got here!"

"I know. But there's nothing wrong with you. I'll get Marvin on the radio and tell him you'll be ready to leave Tuesday."

Dr. Langsom was that way. Very dictatorial. The hospital didn't have direct contact with Selawik because all our radio messages went through Kotzebue. But the message got to Marvin that night via Nome and Kotzebue, that he could pick me up on Tuesday.

Dick Taylor sent word over to Marvin that the ice was piled up on the bar and there was no place to land in Kiana, so Billie lost her chance to see Nome. Marvin routed the youngsters out at four o'clock Tuesday morning, fed them their breakfast, and without washing their faces or combing their hair, poured them into their snowsuits and started for Nome.

Right at seven o'clock, he phoned the hospital. "Get a taxi for Mrs. Warbelow and tell her to be out here at the field in half an hour. It will take me that long to gas."

"Mrs. Warbelow hasn't even been released yet," came the calm voice at the other end of the line. "Dr. Langsom won't be on duty until ten-thirty."

Marvin blustered around and insisted they phone the doctor's room.

Doc wasn't very happy at being roused from a sound sleep. "I won't be on duty until ten-thirty, Warbelow, and it will probably be eleven before I'll have her released."

"But you told me I could pick her up Tuesday morning."

"I didn't expect you to get up in the middle of the night and be here at this hour."

"Well, whose wife is she anyway?" Marvin wanted to know. "I can't fool around here all day. Weather is closing in and I've got to get out of here."

Dr. Langsom wouldn't be budged. "If weather is that bad, you'd better plan to stay over until tomorrow. I don't want that baby sitting out on some mountaintop all night."

So Marvin walked the kids up and down Main Street and browsed through stores for a couple of hours before he came out to the hospital.

Dr. Langsom, whose schedule was dictated by professional demands, didn't arrive a minute ahead of time, and then he sat for nearly a half hour giving me elaborate instructions about formula and the raising of a baby, as any doctor should do.

But then when he began to think about having to face Marvin out in the waiting room, he got a little concerned. "Do you suppose Marvin might be mad at me?" he asked.

I had to admit that I thought he probably would be, so Doctor said maybe he could scrounge up some suckers for the two little ones.

By the time we got out to the waiting room, Marvin had cooled off considerably, and my two dirty-faced little offspring were pleased with their lollipops. I was so happy to see my family after those eight days, that I forgot all else.

Finally, Marvin asked rather emphatically, "Lou, when do we get to see the new baby?"

I hadn't given that a thought. Charlie was still all bundled up on my bed back in my room.

If that baby had waited another couple of days, we would have been in real trouble. There had been a week of warm weather; and although the ice was still firm and dry in the middle of the river in front of the school at Selawik, there was two feet of overflow fifty feet wide along each edge. Ray Skin met us at the plane in hip boots, carrying another pair of boots for Marvin. The three children and I had to be carried from the plane to shore.

The next day Marvin made one last flight to Kotzebue for a load of gas, and the day after that the ice went out.

Marvin Warbelow, left, and passengers on the old Tetlin Bridge.

The Warbelow house, left, in Tetlin.

The general store at Tetlin. Chief Peter and wife, Eva, in center.

Marvin Warbelow keeping warm, next to dogfood cooker in native village, while his plane is being "fire-potted" (warmed up).

The Warbelow family, complete.

Flying high over snowy peaks.

Marvin Warbelow and four fine otter pelts.

Dog mushing with body of aircraft in tow.

Remote native cemetery.

Ice fishing at its best. Photo by Art Warbelow.

In the prime of life.

Marvin Warbelow, right, inspects the frame of his passenger's (Everett Costo) make-shift shelter. This shelter is constructed with willow rods bent and intertwined together. Traditionally it would be covered with tarp or animal skins.

The four moose in this picture would offer great opportunity to many outdoorsmen.

Marvin Warbelow, right, and passenger, Everett Costo, prepared to ascend.

Left to right, Jo Laird, Helen Foster, and Marvin Warbelow, after hiking out from the Kink where

Bill Simmons, left, and Bob Roberts, right, with Bob's PA-14 (Family Cruiser).

One of the Warbelow Super Cubs on floats in the Tanana River at Cathedral Bluffs.

Warbelow Super Cub being pulled to the Tanana River at Cathedral Bluffs.

CHAPTER VIII

In June of 1953 we transferred to Tetlin, just 15 miles off the Alaska Highway near Tok Junction. Unfortunately for us, Tetlin was a beautiful little wooded village and we were happy there. As a result, our lives went into a holding pattern for three years when we might better have been getting on with the next project we had in mind. Marvin knew by this time that flying was in his blood, and eventually he would have to pursue it.

That year we became well-acquainted with the Sager family who owned Riverside Lodge on the Highway just a few miles below Midway lake. Their only son, Corky, had learned to fly, and built himself a runway back of the lodge. He complained that his instructor hadn't really taught him the art of flying, so he quite often went up with Marvin for touch-and-go landings, and before another summer rolled around, he bought our plane from us.

Our fourth and last child was due in June of 1954, so the need for another airplane gave us a good excuse to go back to Wisconsin. Marvin lined up another Cessna 170B in Waterloo, Iowa, and the same day that our son Art was born, he left for Waterloo to pick up his plane. The family waited again at my sister's home while he flew back to Northway, battened down the plane, hitchhiked a ride to Whitehorse, and from there flew back to Wisconsin to bring his family home.

That trip was no easier than the one we had made in our first Cessna 170, but at least it was different. Now that we would be living within a few miles of a road, our lives took on a whole new dimension. We would need more vehicles. So with Art just a month old, we brought a whole caravan up the Alaska Highway. I drove a 1954 Buick with a two-wheeled trailer behind it, and Marvin followed me driving a pickup and hauling a small house trailer. Thirteen long, muddy days later we ended our trek at Northway where Marvin had parked the plane on the edge of the runway. We flew on into Tetlin, about fifteen minutes away.

The village was happy to see the new plane on the airstrip, but after an incident with Paul Joe's groceries shortly after its arrival, they weren't sure whether to be impressed by Marvin's preciseness or disgusted with his poor planning.

Paul had a fish camp up at Tetlin Lake a few minutes' flight away and wanted Marvin to drop some groceries for him in order to lighten his sled when he made his move up there by dog team. So with Paul in the seat beside him to drop the sacks he had packed with food, they took off. They located his campsite on the edge of the lake, and made their circle to get lined up for their first drop.

"Now!" Marvin yelled just as he zeroed in on the camp.

Paul pushed his sack through the window, just in time for it to drop right through a water hole he had cut in the ice near shore.

In the fall of 1956 an epidemic of infectious hepatitis ravaged the whole country, and Marvin was one of the victims. For eight days he was deathly sick, and there was no way to get out of the village and to a hospital except to fly himself out. So he passed the crisis before he could get on his feet enough to walk across the village to the airfield. We had moved our Buick from Northway to Tok, so our plan was to fly to Tok, tie down the plane, and drive the car on into Fairbanks. But since we had never had a baby-sitter in Tetlin, Marvin didn't want to leave the four children in the house with someone who might not know how to cope with all the oil pot-burning heaters we had scattered around. So they all went with us.

The young seminary student for the Episcopal church who was in the village that summer helped us get the family across the river and loaded into the plane. He said a little prayer for us just before take-off; and since Marvin had been having fainting spells, I had a wet washcloth in my hand.

"If something happens to me on the way to Tok, just take the plane on to the big field at Tanacross and land it," Marvin instructed me, just as we moved out onto the runway. But he knew when he said it that I didn't have the faintest idea of how to land an airplane.

Once in Fairbanks, we were told definitely that Marvin had a severe case of hepatitis, that he needed bed rest and a high protein diet. We bought a case of fresh eggs and another case of frozen chicken before we left town.

Back at Tok, we discovered it had been cold the night before and the plane wouldn't start. Marvin pulled the car up to the plane, nose to nose. We opened the hood of the car, draped the motor cover over both engines, and sat there running the car motor until its heat had warmed up the plane to the point where we could start it.

We had butchered a pig earlier that fall, and because the freezer we ordered hadn't arrived yet, had taken the meat over to Northway where Emil Hudic, the local storekeeper, put the meat in his freezer for us. So, on our arrival from Tok, Marvin unloaded the family in Tetlin, then flew on to Northway to pick up our supply of pork. That completed, he finally came home, tied down the plane, and went to bed.

Bed rest was out of the question. We had a school to teach, and he taught it, but he felt miserable and exhausted all winter. He didn't do much flying, and what little he did do wasn't very satisfactory.

After a prolonged snowstorm some time during late winter, the village grew concerned about the fate of old Tommy Paul who had gone up to Last Tetlin before the storm to get a new supply of frozen fish from his summer camp. Last Tetlin was ten miles or more away and snow too deep for dog-teaming, so the villagers persuaded Marvin to fly up and check on him. The airstrip was drifted and in poor shape, so the local fellows agreed to shovel off a space long enough for take-off; but their shoveling didn't amount to a lot. Marvin got off all right, dropped food and a note to Tommy who was just sitting out the storm and probably hoping someone would venture up to Last Tetlin with dogs to help him break trail.

The landing back in Tetlin didn't work out. On take-off, Marvin must have hit some frozen snow clods that cracked his landing gear, because when he came in as low as possible over the end of the field on his return, the ski scraped some tall brush and snapped off. All of us standing on the edge of the field saw what happened, but Marvin didn't realize it until he spot landed, started to slow up, and the stub of the broken leg dug into the snow. Like a slow motion movie, the plane turned a gentle somersault into the soft snow, and Marvin hung upside down in midair with his seatbelt fastened.

He was furious. Once free of his belt, he crawled out the door and stepped back to take a disgusted look at his upside-down airplane.

"Another one all smashed to heck!" he stormed, and the rest of us kept a discreet silence.

He circled the plane for a quick inspection of the damage.

"Well, I guess we'd better get to work," he announced to no one in particular.

Everyone went into action. We had heard pilots tell stories about how they did more damage to planes getting back on their gear than they did when they flipped them. That we didn't want to happen. We tied three ropes to the tail — one to pull it forward, and the other two to hold it back once it started its descent. But the only way to start it on its second somersault was to pull down on the nose, and that was too high in the air for anyone to reach. So with a fourth rope in hand, Donald Joe climbed up on Marvin's shoulders and lassoed the nose just under the prop. Then with everyone in the village on one or another of the ropes, we cautiously pulled the nose down and eased the plane back on its gear.

What might be considered minor damage if you're sitting in front of a hanger can easily turn into a major calamity when you're stuck out in village two hundred miles from nowhere. We had a badly bent prop and some wing damage. The prop would have to go to Anchorage to be straightened, and the only way to get it there was to sled it 15 miles down the dogteam trail to Midway Lake on the Alaska Highway where we had our pickup truck parked. No one had been on the trail since the heavy snows, so with two men on snowshoes breaking trail for the dogs, Marvin and three of the village men made the trip. The dog team returned to the village, and the other three fellows drove that long haul of 350 miles over bad roads to Anchorage, waited until the prop was repaired, picked up the necessary parts to repair the wing, and several days later pulled into Midway again. Two teams met them there and brought back the plane parts and the two older men who had made the trip. Marvin walked home.

He had never recovered from the hepatitis. Extreme fatigue, dizziness, sleepiness, and headaches were only part of the miseries that had plagued him all winter. We knew when he started out for Anchorage that he shouldn't be trying to make the trip, and by the time he walked home through that 15 miles of snow on the trail, he was near collapse. I didn't realize what shape he was in until he slumped down in a chair and tears began to roll down his cheeks. He was too choked up to speak, and when he finally asked for a drink of water, he couldn't swallow it.

"This is it!" I decided. "Never again will we get caught in a situation like this. Come spring, we're moving to the highway, and that's that!"

I could safely make that statement, because we had just a few weeks before that, submitted the high bid on an old army base at Cathedral Bluffs, just 25 miles up the Alaska Highway from Tok toward Fairbanks. The place was ours, and we started making plans to move on it as soon as school was out. This location eventually would become Cathedral Bluffs Lodge.

During the early spring, Marvin began making flights on weekends to Midway Lake with our personal belongings where he stored them in the house trailer we had parked there, and by late April we had nothing but our freezable foodstuffs and the family to move out. Breakup was coming earlier than usual, and the airstrip was already in too bad shape for ski take-offs, so we had moved the plane to Skate Lake nearly a half mile from the village.

Marvin got up about four o'clock on Saturday morning in order to make the most use he could of the little bit of freezing he might have gained during the coldest part of the night. The plane was already loaded with nine cases of canned goods and odds and ends of other groceries. He taxied as far to the edge of the lake as he could to get the advantage of every inch of runway, but just as he started to lift off, the skis hit the frozen dogsled trail and a gear snapped. He couldn't tell from the cockpit just what had happened, but the ski was hanging vertically below him and he could hear the tip of it banging on the belly of the fuselage.

He circled the village just once to let someone know what had happened. I thought at first he was simply buzzing the house to say good-bye, but then I realized that the motor was making some strange noises. I jumped out of bed and into a robe; but when I tried to get my feet into a pair of boots, my hands were shaking so badly I couldn't tie the strings. I stumbled out the back door, tripping on boot strings, just in time to meet Titus Paul running around the corner of the house, waving wildly up in the air at the plane, and panting, "Look! His ski, his ski! All we can do now is pray!"

"Titus!" I yelled back at him, "while you're praying, run for the lake as fast as you can. Somebody's got to be there when he tries to land."

Titus disappeared around the corner again without a word. I managed to wad up my shoestrings enough to keep from tripping again, and followed him full-speed down the trail to the lake. By this time everyone in the village was piling out of cabin doors in every stage of dress and undress with uncombed hair flying in all directions. Within two or three minutes fifty people had converged on the trail; and breaking through soft snow and slush at every step, we moved like an army of ants on the march toward Skate Lake.

Marvin, in the meantime, was doing some fast thinking. His first thought was to head right for Northway where there was a CAA station and access to the highway and a doctor. But when he thought of crash-landing on a plowed runway with nine cases of canned goods tumbling down on him, he squashed that plan and changed his course, heading for Midway Lake. He thought he might be able to get a door open, push his load a box at a time out of the plane, and make an easier landing on the soft deep snow of the lake.

But within a matter of minutes, he realized his motor was laboring and heating up so fast he would never make Midway. So he banked, made as short a turn as he dared, and started back to Tetlin. By the time he reached Skate Lake he could see a long fringe of bodies lining the shore, and knew that at least he had plenty of help, whatever happened.

Somewhere along the way, the ski had finally dropped off, so all he had to contend with was another stub of the axle. But this time he knew he was missing a ski, so when he glided in to land, he held the gear up until he could touch down on a spot of bare ice. The stub dug in, but he had dissipated enough speed so that he managed to stay upright. The plane made a half turn, and settled down on one wingtip.

Annie Joe, a lady who lived at the far end of the village, for some reason didn't get into action as fast as the rest of us did. So after the excitement had died down and all fifty or so of us started back down the trail to the village, Annie was standing wide-eyed just a couple of feet off the trail, staring at every person one at a time, as he went by her. Marvin was just ahead of me. She gave him a long, astonished look as he went past her. Then, as I came up next, she gasped, "Warbelow 'live again!"

We, of course, were now in another predicament. We still sat in Tetlin with the plane out of commission.

Fortunately, Corky Sager came in about an hour later to pick up a visiting missionary he had flown in the day before. His plane was still on skis, so he went back to Riverside to pick up his wheels. But they wouldn't fit our plane, so he and Marvin made another trip to Midway and brought back our own set of wheels. Together they put the wheels on our plane and did what they could to toggle up the damaged wingtip, and decided that with the warm weather and rapidly deteriorating ice, it was now or never. If we weren't out of there the next morning, we were going to be sitting in Tetlin until the last part of May.

It never got below freezing that night. By 2 a.m. the sun with its devastating heat was already sneaking above the horizon, so Marvin, on wheels, plowed through a rapidly growing lake of slush, and lifted off Skate Lake for the last time.

Two hours later, Corky, with the little silver 170 that had carried us from Wisconsin to Selawik four years earlier, landed on what remained of the ice on Skate Lake. I had the four children up and dressed; and with a minimum of luggage that literally amounted to one change of clothes apiece for them, we had our last dog team ride from the village to the lake. Corky, in his usual easy-going loose-jointed manner, buckled us down into our seats.

Knowing full well that he had a load, that we had nothing but a foot of slush on top of a layer of rotting ice beneath us, and a short lake with a forest of trees ahead of us, Corky belted himself into his seat. That typical twisted smile of his never left his face as he turned the switch, watched the prop speed up into a whir of nothingness, and then glanced sidewise at me with a casual, "Well, I guess we're ready to take off."

We plunged into a mass of water that completely blinded us, the plane plowed and bumpity-bumped its way across the lake. We lifted, and just as he dipped a wing suddenly to avoid a treetop on the other side, Corky drawled, "Kinda bumpy take-off." Corky certainly had learned the art of flying!

Although the 170 had made it from Tetlin to Riverside on its own power, it needed repair. Corky recommended that we take it to Delta to Art Smith, who had done work on Corky's plane.

"He's a dern good mechanic, Marv," Corky insisted.

We needed a couple of days to get our trailer and the buick shoveled out of the snowdrifts at Midway Lake, and moved them to a homestead we had taken up on the Highway just five miles out of Tok. Cathedral Bluffs was even more snowed-in, and it would be some time before we could get a generator set up there and enough snow moved to make the place habitable.

Once we were settled in the trailer, the children and I drove the car to Delta, 115 miles toward Fairbanks, and Marvin flew the plane. That day we had our first meeting with the Art Smith family.

Art was a tall, prematurely white-haired, striking man with a wonderful flair for story-telling. His wife, Betty, a jovial little red-headed nurse, herded her family of four youngsters, all under five years old, around the house like the voice of experience. And all the while, she was perking coffee, cutting chocolate cake, and chattering with her guests. Theirs was a house where everyone stopped just in passing by, and no one stood on ceremony. By the time the coffee was ready, there were four pilots and ten kids there.

Art looked the plane over, and determined what repairs he would need to replace damaged parts, and at the same time do a hundred-hour inspection on it. We drove on into Fairbanks and Marvin picked up the list of parts. But when we got back to Delta Art found out someone had sold us filed-down points when we had paid for new ones. So Marvin made another trip back to Fairbanks and got the matter straightened out.

With the plane finally back in shape, Marvin brought it home and tied it down on the Tok airstrip. But a few days later when he decided to fly back into Tetlin to pick up our mail, he found six holes in one of the wings. An ambitious woodpecker had walked right down the center and pecked a hole into every rib. The trip was delayed while he came home for patching material.

CHAPTER IX

It was June before we had our new home at Cathedral Bluffs liveable. The Bluffs was an unusual spot. The installation had been built for the Army by the Alaska Communications System (ACS). It included a communications building 106 feet long and 20 feet wide, a bachelor's quarters (BQ), several other out-buildings, and a beautiful three-bedroom house that had been the home of the commanding officer. The station had been used only two years when the military decided radio reception was poor there and they moved into Tok. The whole place was boarded up, and it was at this point that we took over. We were within 100 feet of the Alaska Highway, with the Alaska Range right across the road from us and the Tanana River boiling past us on the other side, not more than a city block from our back door.

The only possible spot for an airstrip was a thousand foot stretch that parallelled the long, gradual hill on the Highway in front of our property. But we had no heavy equipment with which to build any kind of a landing strip, so the plane stayed at the Tok airstrip for the next year and a half.

A construction crew, rebuilding a series of small bridges along the road from Cathedral Bluffs to Delta moved in shortly after we opened our new place. Marvin went to work as a laborer and stayed with them for two summers. We spent our evenings and weekends tearing apart and rebuilding that huge communications building, and by the end of the summer we had the makings of a roadhouse, typical of all those that were scattered along the Alaska Highway during the era after the building of the road.

Marvin enjoyed his work. He made more money swinging a shovel than he and I together had made teaching school. An eight to five job with no responsibilities after hours was a real treat. So when Bill Adams, the one-man representative of the Bureau of Land Management (BLM) at Tanacross, began to talk to him about getting himself a commercial license and an air taxi business, Marvin wasn't interested.

"Look, Bill," he argued, "I've got it made. On construction I know I'm going to be bringing in nine hundred a month, and the responsibility of the business is someone else's headache. An air taxi would be too much of a gamble, and I have four kids to support."

"Marvin, if you get yourself licensed, I'll guarantee you that with the flying I can give you, you can pay for a new plane in one season."

Although Marvin didn't take that too seriously, he did go right on buying and selling airplanes. The next spring he sold the 170 to a serviceman from Eielson Air Base. The young man didn't have the $2800 we wanted for it, so he gave us a set of encyclopedias as part payment. Some book salesman must have made a real killing on the base because every G.I. on Eielson had a set just like it.

Then began more evening sessions with "Trade-A-Plane", and phone calls to sellers all over the States. By April we had located a 170B in Indiana, and he left for another trip south to pick it up.

The Vern Johnson family in Tok quite often drove to Cathedral on a Sunday afternoon to exchange gossip and give our youngsters a chance to play together. Vern wasn't at all surprised when they arrived the Sunday after Marvin left. "I knew that old horse-trader Warbelow couldn't get along without a plane," he declared.

Two weeks later Marvin and our nephew Pete Bodette from Wisconsin arrived in our new plane.

Pete, just twenty-one years old, was all wound up, since he had never been in Alaska before.

"That was *some* trip! The only trouble was you couldn't get Marvin to stop long enough any place to get something to eat. I about starved to death. Then when we got to Fort Nelson, we finally had a square meal and I got a shower. But Marvin was too tired to shower that night, so said he'd wait until morning. Well, the next morning there wasn't any hot water, and did he ever hit the ceiling!"

"That's par for the course," I recalled. "We didn't have any hot water in Fort Nelson five years ago, either."

A good-sized construction company moved into Cathedral Bluffs that spring to do a half-sole blacktop job on the Alaska Highway. They took over the entire lodge, put in their own power plant for the summer, cleared off a trailer parking area on the lower end of the property, and moved in about twenty families. We not only had people living in every available building we had, but we even rented our comfortable home to one of the foremen, and squeezed our family into our little 21-foot trailer for the season.

Marvin worked that summer again on the bridge crew and Pete went with him. The kids and I ran the gas pumps, and I even moved our little grocery store into the basement of the house. That was a wild summer for the family, but the plane spent most of the time tied down in Tok.

Part of our arrangement with the construction company was that they would doze out an airstrip for us while they were there. But the summer turned out to be an endless round of bickering between us, and they changed their minds about the strip. However, when they moved their crew out in mid-September, their operator's foreman stayed behind a few days to pick up the loose ends. He took the attitude that a bargain was a bargain; so before he left, he dozed out a thousand foot strip for us beside the highway, reaching from the gas pumps and telephone wires at the upper end to the bridge at the lower.

About two-thirds of the way down the strip, we had a ridge that reached all the way across it. The bump turned out to be quite an asset. It was just at the point where a plane had to be ready to fly, and that hump gave it the extra boost it needed.

During hunting season that fall, various groups of sheep hunters stopped in for gas, and Marvin began to perk up his ears at some of the hunting stories he heard.

"Do you know, we're sitting right here in some of the best sheep hunting spots in the country. Now if a fellow just had an airplane and an air taxi license..."

While he was beginning to think along these lines, someone threw another bait at him. He had been promoted to steel worker and was still on the job with the bridge crew. The company wanted to bid on a new job coming up at Skagway, so they made a deal with Marvin. If he would fly three of their men to Haines and Skagway, they'd keep him on the payroll, and pay all his expenses. He took them up on it.

That trip was just what Marvin needed, for a couple of reasons. They got as far as Haines without incident, but then flew on to Skagway to look at the job down there and got weathered in for five days. Nothing could have suited Marvin better. He was tired out from a summer of long hours on the job plus trying to run the operation at Cathedral. He crawled into bed and literally slept those five days, getting out only long enough to eat a meal. The only diversion he had was the 3 a.m. parties they had when one of the fellows came in every night with a case of beer and another case of tomato juice and woke up his three fellow travelers.

Marvin came home looking more rested than he had in years. The calluses were all gone from his hands and the circles under his eyes had disappeared. But the King for a Day got back into the groove real quick.

The next day they poured cement.

Our little 170 didn't go back to the Tok airstrip again. Marvin did some more work on the runway, we picked up rocks and cut brush along the edges, and at long last had an airfield of our own. Over the next few years the road proved to be a better landing strip than the field did, but at least it was a good place to tie down.

By now Marvin had definitely decided that a commercial license was the way to go. In the fall of 1957 we sold the 170 to Floyd Miller at Northway who was in a neck-to-neck race with us to see who could get licensed first. He, too, intended to become a commercial pilot.

With the plane out of the way, we made another trip to the lower states that fall and Marvin flew his next bird, a 170B (4404

Bravo) up from Dallas, Texas. He spent long hours that winter with his Jeppesen manual, and by spring was ready for his written test. Interest ran high in the neighborhood, as Tok had never had a commercial pilot before. He had already agreed to do the BLM flying for the summer, and the rest of the community was pushing him.

The nurse called one day. "Will you have your commercial by Friday so I can fly into Tetlin?" she wanted to know.

Two fellows from Tok made a trip up to Cathedral Bluffs to inquire about the possibility of taking flying lessons, and asked if Marvin would have his instructor's license. One of them had already bought himself a plane. And Bob Greene, the missionary from Tanacross, called to say that the Businessmen's Association had decided to push hunting and fishing in the area that summer, and they would be needing a pilot for fly-in fishermen.

Marvin was making all kinds of promises to everyone, with no idea at all as to whether he would be able to keep them. But in April he passed his written test with an 80% — quite a disappointment for me who thought I would be able to write home that he had passed with a perfect score.

The flight test was a little more rugged. One day in May he left for Fairbanks all dressed up, clean-shaven, and his hair combed. Three days later he came home with stubble on his chin, circles under his eyes, and his clothes ready for the washing machine. But he had his license.

Fire season got Marvin off to a good start. It was dry that summer, and the BLM was in its heyday money-wise, so *Warbelow's Air Ventures'* only pilot began to pile up hours doing fire patrol. This was the only job Marvin had had in a long time when he could dress up to go to work. I hadn't seen him so slick and polished-looking in years. One day he flew from 11 a.m. until 5 a.m. the next morning with only short rests in between and grossed four hundred dollars. We had never seen that much money for a day's work in our lives.

About that time we had an abrupt reminder of just what's involved in the flying game. Corky Sager got himself wound up in his prop.

The morning of his accident, Pop Cosgrove in Delta saw Corky's plane in the air. And since Corky hadn't flown it that morning, they assumed someone from a construction crew headquartered there had helped himself to a free ride. Whoever had taken it, left the master switch on.

Later that day, Corky decided to take some friends up for a flight. The plane had to be hand-propped, and with just one flip, he had had it. It broke the bones all across his left hand and cut the ligaments in his right elbow. The prop caught his pants across his thighs and burned and gashed both legs. He spent two weeks in the hospital, then stopped by with his dad to visit us on his way back to his home at Riverside Lodge to recuperate and rest. He had his left hand and right arm in casts, and I fed him his breakfast spoonful by spoonful. Shortly after that, he was back in the hospital with blood poisoning in his elbow, but Corky wasn't one to be easily held down. Two weeks later he was driving his fuel truck back and forth between Valdez and Tok.

The flying would have been a lot easier for Marvin had that been all he had to do. But it seemed that every night he came home only to face a mound of problems that had accumulated during the day at the Lodge or some of the outbuildings. A lot of road and bridge construction was going on along the Alaska Highway, and that summer we had a crew of ten or twelve bridge workers living in the bunkhouse. Rascal, the cook, worked on the job all day, then tied a red kerchief around his head and doubled as a cook after hours.

Marvin had had two long days of flying. One day he flew fire patrol from five to five. The next day he did a trip to Northway with the state welfare worker, and another one to Tetlin with Bob Greene and some government personnel from Juneau. Bush pilots had a habit of going without food all day, once they left home base. So he rolled in about dinnertime tired and hungry, only to be met by half the bridge crew before he could get out of the plane. They had been to Tok for groceries, all got drunk with the exception of two clean-cut young Mormon boys who had managed to herd them home. But now their oil-fired range was acting up and they couldn't cook a meal. By the time Marvin got his plane tied down and walked to the bunkhouse, they were in a real mess.

There on the work table was a stack of chops and big thick steaks. Rascal and his kitchen helpers were milling around like a herd of reindeer, all half starved, but nobody sober enough to know what to do about it. Someone had managed to put a pot of potatoes on the cold stove, hoping it would boil, but hadn't covered it. And someone else was running around with a coffee pot in his hand. Rascal was busy bragging about all this $32 worth of meat and hot biscuits he was going to cook, but not getting any of it done. Marvin spent two hours draining water out of the oil lines and tinkering with the carburetor before I finally went down to see what had happened to him. Next morning we asked the inspector who bunked and batched in the building next door how they fared that night, and he said that by ten-thirty Rascal had a regular banquet on the table.

In August, Chief Peter Joe passed away in Tetlin. Chief had suffered a stroke and had been in the Tanana Hospital for some time. When it became obvious that he could never recover, they flew him home to be with his wife and family those last days. He had been a strong leader in his younger days, and his passing was a real loss to the village.

Chief was a very special man, and his funeral a very special affair. His was one of the first commercial caskets ever to come into the village. Friends and relatives from all the surrounding villages gathered in Tetlin to see him while he was still living, and then stayed on for the funeral.

Funerals are traditionally followed by several days of potlatch, visiting, and gift-exchanging, but for lack of fresh meat, Chief's potlatch was delayed until the last part of September. The fellows at Tetlin shot a moose, so the guests returned and remembered Chief again in the lighter tone of the potlatch.

With guests coming from as far away as Minto and Tanana, Marvin, Corky, and Floyd Miller all did an amazing amount of flying over a period of several days.

CHAPTER X

We had turned down a few chances to fly fishermen into lakes off the highway; so when things began to slow up in the late fall of 1958, we had time to discuss the possibilities of a float plane. Marvin was still thinking completely in terms of another 170. Art Smith discouraged him on this. Art had flown a 170 on floats and didn't like it. Under-powered, he said.

That story didn't stop us. We turned to "Trade-A-Plane" again and answered ad after ad, first trying to locate just a pair of floats. But by the time our letters reached their destinations, the floats were always already gone. "People must have money," Marvin decided. "A pair of floats costs from $1200 to $2000.

We finally gave up on the idea of pontoons and began looking for a 170 with floats already mounted. We found exactly two — one in Ketchikan and the other in Toronto. The Ketchikan plane was a 1956 model owned by some fellow named Jack. After several phone calls back and forth, the two men decided to close the deal. But Ketchikan has open water year round, and the plane was being used all winter, so it would be April before we could have it.

"I don't know just how I'll get it up here," Marvin commented. "We have two problems. First, I don't have my float license, and second, there's no place up here in April to land on floats. I'll either have to have Jack fly it up for me or I'll go down there and get my license while I'm in Ketchikan. Then I can fly as far as Haines and tie down until rivers and lakes open up here."

He mailed a check to Jack with a long line of stipulations on the back of it, and immediately began to make commitments for float flying with the BLM for the summer. So it was quite a jolt when the check was returned and Jack said he wasn't going to sign his name to a whole string of stuff that would eventually end up in court. We decided to take a chance on the condition of the plane, and sent him another check minus the stipulations.

In the meantime, Jack had a chance to lease the plane for the summer and it sounded like a better deal to him than selling it, so he wrote us a refund check, saying he had changed his mind. By this time we had lost our chance to have the plane in Toronto and we were already committed to a summer of flying, so Marvin phoned him.

"You can't do this to me, Jack. We made a deal, I paid you the money, and I have contracted for float flying this summer. I've lost my chance to buy any other plane I had on the string because I assumed I had yours."

Jack wouldn't budge. So when Marvin insisted it was either let us have the plane or get a lawyer, he said, "Go ahead. Get your lawyer."

We did. For two hundred dollars a lawyer in Fairbanks contacted Jack's lawyer in Ketchikan and they decided we did have a legal agreement. Jack of course, wasn't pleased. The original agreement had been that we pick up the plane any time after April 20, but in view of the latest developments, he said the plane would have to be claimed on April 20, or not at all.

This put us in a spot. Marvin looked over the river situation at Tanacross and decided that there was a small open spot of water he could set down in. Just to be sure he wasn't going to miss his date, he went to Fairbanks and flew to Ketchikan two days early. Jack had taken off for Seattle and didn't go back to Ketchikan until Marvin was out of town. Marvin picked up his plane, hired an instructor to give him a couple of hours of instruction, and then headed north. At Haines he hired a fellow to drill a hole through the cover of the gas tank. He bought 30 gallons of fuel in five-gallon jeep cans, a hand pump, and a plastic hose. With the jeep cans in the plane, he put one end of the hose through the gas cap, ran it through a crack in the window, and gassed the plane in midair all the way from Haines to Tanacross.

Mrs. Sager called me that afternoon from Riverside Lodge about fifty miles below us. "We just saw a float plane going over. Do you think that could mean anything?"

I was petrified, because during the few days after Marvin left for Ketchikan, the temperature had dropped to twenty below a couple of nights, and I was sure his open spot in the river at Tanacross must have frozen over.

Bob Greene, who lived in the village of Tanacross on the far side of the river, spotted the plane circling, and immediately called Bill Adams, who lived on the opposite side of the river.

"Bill, do you see that float plane up there? It must be some crazy tourist from the lower states who thinks summer has come."

Well, the river hadn't frozen over, and Marvin did manage to set down. It happened to be somebody's birthday over at the Adams house, so we all congregated there and helped finish out the birthday party before we began to figure out what we would do with the plane until the ice melted.

Keeping the float plane on the river at Tanacross twelve miles down the highway from us, or at Moon Lake, six miles away was time-consuming and costly. So we had no choice but to park it on the Tanana River right back of the lodge. There were plenty of headaches with that, too. We had a series of rapids in that part of the river, so water was always turbulent. And with the river's rising and falling with every rainstorm, we were constantly pulling the plane further up on shore or pushing it down into the river. At extremely high water times we had to move it upstream a couple of blocks into a small slough. And if the water chose to recede during the night, the next morning our floats would be stuck in the muck of the slough.

We did take a few fishing parties out that summer, though. And the Tanacross people who usually boated to their summer fishing camp up at Mansfield Lake found out it was easier to pay six dollars for a flight back there, rather than deal with a boat.

Carl Charles from Dot Lake dropped by quite often. He told us stories about a lake he had located back in the hills from Dot Lake where he had found some peculiar fish, and finally convinced Marvin that they should do a little investigating. They went in one day with the floats, and came back with a bag full of strange things they called bull trout. These fish had oversized heads suggestive of bullheads and smaller trout-like bodies, with a definite trout taste. The Fish and Game boys later determined that they were a stunted trout of some sort, living in a lake overpopulated with fish and lacking in food.

The Fish and Game Commission had a big re-stocking program going on that summer, so Marvin spent considerable time in the air with the local biologists. They filled balloon-type plastic bags full of tiny fish, flew over the lakes to be stocked, and dropped their bags. The bags broke on impact; and although a lot of the babies never survived that blow, enough of them lived so that today those lakes are well-populated with harvestable fish.

By this time, the federal government had set the wheels in motion to withdraw huge masses of land in Alaska for national parks, and the state was to have first choice as to what land we wanted to keep. We flew surveyors into the back country off the highway to plot out their lands, and that too, had to be done by float plane.

Wiens had for years flown the mail twice monthly from Fairbanks into Tetlin. In the summer of 1959, the Post Office Department decided to cancel that contract and fly it out of Tok. It was a lot cheaper to bring it overland on a mail bus from Fairbanks to Tok, since the bus was coming anyway. We bid the new contract in for $18.75 a round trip, twice monthly, and got it. There again, we had problems. We lived 25 miles from Tok and had no vehicle down there to transport mail two miles between the airstrip and post office. Right across the road from the post office was the Alaska Road Commission complex, with a nice wide ditch in front of it.

Marvin went to the state trooper. "Tom, I've got a problem. I don't have a vehicle here in Tok, and even if I parked one out at the airstrip, during the winter I couldn't get it started. But I could land in that ditch right across from the post office and pick up my mail. What do you say?"

Tom drove out to look over the situation. "Well, it looks like a pretty good landing spot to me. I guess as long as you can get in and out of there without letting your wing hang over the highway, I'd have no objection."

That worked for a while, but then a local airstrip owner objected because he wanted to collect his two dollars for each landing and take-off. One day while the plane was parked for the mail pickup, he phoned the trooper.

"Warbelow's plane is out here again, and you can't tell me it isn't blocking half the road!"

Trooper Tom went out for another inspection. It was quite evident that we had a marginal operation. But they noted that right along the edge of the ditch was a road commission sign. So instead of Marvin's being banned from the ditch, Tom asked the ARC if they would move their sign in order to give the plane a little more room. The men liked the excitement of seeing the plane land, so the sign came down.

CHAPTER XI

Our sources of revenue and the extent of the flying *Warbelow's Air Ventures* would be doing began to fall into place. We got a good share of our business from the state Fish and Game Service. Up until now they hadn't done a great deal of aerial work on animal counts, but new programs were rapidly opening up. The 170 on wheels checker-boarded vast areas of the 40-Mile country, counting moose population, caribou, Dall sheep, and even beaver.

The word 40-Mile was derived from the 40-Mile River that flowed through the mass of land that stretched from Tok to Eagle and on up toward Dawson City.

The store in Tetlin had for years freighted its own groceries up the Tanana and Tetlin rivers from the Alaska Highway, where they picked their goods up from a truck out of Anchorage. The system hadn't been very successful. Roads were bad and communication the same. Every fall it seemed a crew from the village went down river with the boat, only to sit at the bridge for several days waiting for the truck to arrive. That, plus the usual breakdowns along the river once they were loaded, made the situation worse.

Even during the years we lived at Tetlin, Marvin could see other possibilities for getting those groceries in more economically, and now of course he wanted the business himself. He made a trip over to the village to talk to the Council.

"Look, you guys. Why not lay up that boat and forget about feeding a crew of men sitting down there at the steel bridge for days every fall. I'll fly that freight in for you from Cathedral Bluffs cheaper than you can bring it up yourselves. Nobody needs to wait for the truck to come. Whenever it gets here, we can unload the groceries into my garage where I can keep it from freezing until I can get it in here. You won't be limited to just one order a year when the river is navigable. Split your orders up into smaller ones and we'll bring them in any time you want."

They were sold on the idea, and for the next several years, we handled tons of freight for Tetlin. Usually the orders were limited to three or four thousand pounds, but I remember one Christmas Eve, at fifty below, the truck pulled in with eleven thousand pounds.

The freight usually got flown into Tetlin the day after it arrived. We'd load our two-ton truck with boxes and take it to Tok. While Marvin flew a load of groceries into the village, the kids and I would pile up a second load for him beside the truck. We shortly became experts at estimating. We could almost guess how many small, heavy boxes plus a few light, bulky ones we could stack up in order to make a planeload with both the right volume and weight. We'd start our operation as early in the morning as we could, and usually spent most of the day getting it delivered. A few passengers on backhauls boosted our revenue.

"I like this kind of flying," Marvin often said. "Freight never talks back to you."

What in a short time mushroomed into the most lucrative and intensive flying time of the year began that fall of 1959 when hunters started inquiring into the possibilities of flying into the hills for moose and sheep. We operated with just two Cessnas, one on wheels, the other on floats during the summer, and both of them on skis come winter. It wasn't until three years later that we finally acquired our first Super Cub, and from then on, the Dall sheep hunting overshadowed moose and caribou.

That first year, we tried offering a package deal of $100 to take a man hunting and bring his meat out. But that wasn't very practical. Since we were dealing mainly with moose hunters, the meat was a major item. Some fellows boned their meat and brought out just what they could use, but others brought it out bones and all. Most hunters wanted their horns, although a few left them behind. Some wanted the hides, and a few wanted the whole head. So we changed the package. Marvin flew a hunter into his spot round

90

trip for $35 and then flew his meat and horns out for fifteen cents a pound. Marvin chose the spot, and the $35 was the same regardless of the length of the flight. The hunter could use his own judgment as to how much meat he wanted to pay to haul. With that kind of a plan, he did a lot more trimming on the spot.

The last of the hunters quite often got caught in the first snowstorm of the season and we'd have to get a plane on skis to get them out.

That winter, flying was miserable. We had a pair of wheel skis for one plane, but used conventional skis on the second one. The straight skis were a lot lighter and we could use that plane to get into tighter spots. But we had our headaches with them. They froze down to the ground if they sat flat, so every day after the last flight, we'd have to put two-by-fours under each ski to keep it free of ice. If we didn't have an accumulation of fresh snow on the wings every morning, we could at least be sure we'd have frost that stuck tight. These were dangerous situations that could lead to accidents. Every morning two of us would see-saw back and forth the entire length of each wing with an old all-wool blanket until we had the wing free of ice and snow.

But the most miserable part of winter flying was the fire-potting. For at least an hour every morning, Marvin had to sit under a greasy tarp draped over the fuselage with a propane firepot beside him blazing away to heat up the motor. He wore the same old greasy parka every day for this session and then changed to his clean one when he got ready to fly. More than once his ruff or the cuff of his parka caught fire, and if he dared take time out to come inside for a quick breakfast, someone had to stand guard at a window to be sure the whole tarp didn't go up in flames. Our planes were tied in sort of a circle around the front yard, and as the years went by and planes were added to the fleet, we just increased the size of the circle.

We were always looking for an easier way to heat the motors, and little by little our situation improved; Marvin designed a horseshoe-shaped heater that fitted right around the nose of the plane. With both ends open, the heat blew from the center of the horseshoe directly through the open grillwork of the nose into the motor. He sent his plans to a welding shop down in the lower

91

states and had two of these heaters made up. They served well for years.

Then some time later, a compact little heater not any bigger around than a dinner plate came on to the market. It could be placed right under the cowling and rested on the motor, and was safe to be left in overnight.

Instruments wouldn't operate when they were frozen, so while the motor was being heated, we'd have an electric heater turned on inside the cabin. Those heaters were dangerous, too. Floyd Miller burned up a whole plane one morning when his heater tipped over on the seat down at Northway.

During those short days in December and January, a pilot had to take off and land in the dark if he were going to get in any flying at all. The ARC fellows coming home from a day of shoveling or thawing culverts along the highway, usually passed Cathedral about the time Marvin's lights were twinkling off in the distance. When that happened, they would pull up and watch while he settled in, lined up for a landing, and his landing light came on to flood the short strip paralleling the highway. They'd sit right there until the plane had come to a halt and taxied into its parking place.

"That sure looks romantic!" one of them sighed over a cup of coffee at the counter in our cafe.

"Not as romantic as it looks," Marvin assured him. "It's just a glorified truck driver's job."

I don't think most people had any idea of the miserable hours we spent getting planes ready to go in the morning and putting them to bed at night. The boys stood on oil drums every evening after dinner and filled gas tanks with five gallon jeep cans. The last thing Marvin did at night was to make the rounds checking tiedowns. Several times a winter, we would have a chinook wind that turned into a miniature cyclone rolling down off the Alaska Range and lasting for hours. On those nights, the whole family would be out hanging on to wings or rolling up additional drums of oil to reinforce tiedowns on the wings or make extra tiedowns for the tail sections. And on those nights when Marvin was overdue, it was a game with the kids to stand at the windows and see who could first spot a small twinkle from the navigation lights breaking that eternal darkness. If they stood there long enough, the light usually appeared, but once in awhile it didn't.

We were well past the peak of moose-hunting season when Marvin crippled the float plane. He had wedged a litle hunting of his own in between flying out other hunters, and shot a moose on a small lake several miles back of Mansfield Lake. The lake he had landed on was shaped like an hourglass, and neither part of it was long enough for take-off. He had to start his take-off on one half of the hourglass, get up on the step as he was going through the narrow neck, and lift off on the second half of the lake. This worked fine when he brought in his first load of meat. But when he went back for his last load, wind conditions had changed. With a head wind, the plane was ready to lift just as it went through the narrow neck, and Marvin let it have its own way. But once off the water, it wasn't so easy to control. A gust of wind knocked it off course and one wing got caught in the shoreline trees. Marvin had to set down again, and that was it. The plane was far too damaged to consider another attempt at flight.

He tied the plane down with the meat still in it, and started walking. When it got so dark he couldn't see any more, he curled up squirrel-fashion under a tree and shivered until daylight. Late September is right on the edge of winter, and it was no time for boy-scouting. Some time the next forenoon he reached Mansfield Lake where we had already started to set up a fishing camp, so we had our aluminum boat and ten-horse motor stashed there. Buck Stewart, the game warden, had established a camp right next to ours. He had some gas and a can of baked beans at his site; so with the gas, beans, boat and motor, Marvin got himself to Tanacross by mid-afternoon.

He had told me more than once that if he ever failed to come home from a flight, we should give him twenty-four hours before we sounded the alarm. But I never paid any attention to that. When he didn't show up at daylight, I called Bob and Ellis Roberts. Their float plane was tied down on the Tanana River somewhere back off the highway, so they loaded up a pickup with gas and headed for the river. They flew the area where I thought

Marvin might be down, but didn't locate the plane, and came back to Tok just about the time Marvin boated into Tanacross.

Marvin was lame, tired, and hungry, but there wasn't any time to rest. He had several hunters sitting out in the hills, and no plane with which to bring them in. The next morning he flew over each hunting camp with the wheel plane to drop notes and tell them to sit tight until he could get in for them. That same day he phoned every air service in Fairbanks, and by a streak of luck was able to locate a Taylorcraft on floats that had just been recovered. The job had cost more than the owner could afford. He couldn't even redeem his plane, so had it up for sale. The next day Marvin went to town and brought home the little two-place T-Craft on floats.

Art Smith came to Cathedral Bluffs from Delta and Corky Sager from Riverside Lodge. With three heads together they came up with a variety of solutions to the recovery of Cessna 3479 Delta, none of which materialized. Marvin had flown over to the hourglass lake from Tanacross and knew he had a water route the entire way. Questionable in places it was, with full-grown windfalls crossing the rivers, snags, stumps, and even a couple of set nets the Mansfield people had put out.

"It would take several days to clear a waterway, but I think we could do it before freeze-up and then just taxi the plane on floats all the way to Tanacross," Marvin suggested.

"Heck, no!" Art protested. "You'd rip the bottoms right off the floats with all that garbage in them cricks. That's a bum idea, Marv. Personally, I think a fellow could go in there with a pair of tin snips and some screws and toggle that wing up enough to ferry it out of there."

"Gol dern, if the wing is as bad as Marv says it is, I wouldn't want to be the guy to fly it out," was Corky's opinion.

"It's that bad, all right," Marvin agreed. "If we're going to fly it out, there's no way but to get a whole new wing, and I don't know how we'd get the wing up there."

"Of course there's another way," Art volunteered. "We could wait until freeze-up and then bring my weasel down from Delta and haul it out."

But shortly after that Art got hit with a case of flu that lasted for weeks, and the float plane sat out in the buckbrush until the next spring.

Corky had had his problems, too. Art had for some time flown his fishermen into Summit Lake with an old 1933 Stinson he had bought from Lon Brennan at Manley Hot Springs, and called it Junior. He talked a lot about recovering it with metal, and no one really believed he would ever do it. But one winter, sure enough, he ripped it all down and the next spring when the shop door opened, out rolled that shiny metal plane like a newborn butterfly out of its cocoon.

About this time Art decided to put his flying career on hold and go into partnership in an aircraft maintenance shop in Anchorage. He offered Junior for sale to the first man who appeared with money in hand.

But he ran into trouble locating housing in Anchorage. There were plenty of three-bedroom houses for rent, but all with stipulations of no children or pets. Furthermore, since he had always worked alone, he was having second thoughts about joining a partnership.

In the meantime, Corky had fallen in love with Junior and was the first person to appear with money in hand. Art had, by this time, made up his mind not to sell; but he kept his word, and Junior was passed on to Corky.

One of Corky's first trips with his new plane was to take two loads of fishermen up into the Nabesna country. He managed to get his first load back out at the end of their fishing trip, but Junior refused to start when it was time for the second trip. Marvin finally went in to bring the last load of hunters out, and Corky called Art down to find out what had gone wrong with Junior. Art's conclusion was that the engine had been flooded.

Marvin had taken a look at the plane when he brought out that second load of fishermen, and he had little hopes for it. So when Corky called the next day to say that it was flying again, Marvin was impressed.

"What did Art do to it, anyway?" he asked.

"Wal," Corky replied, "I think that dern thing was afraid

of him!''

Marvin's first trip into Canada proved to be quite a hassle. He was supposed to go to Dawson City to pick up two Catholic nuns. There was so much red tape connected with it that it took Marvin and the FAA at Northway two days just to get all the arrangements made. Then when he got to Dawson, it turned out that one of the nuns was an American, but the other a Canadian; and Canada had a regulation that an American plane couldn't come into Canada and transport a Canadian out of the country. They almost refused to let the Canadian go, but since her flying partner was American, they finally decided to close their eyes and let her sneak out.

Flying all the way down to Northway to go through American Customs on the return trip involved an extra hour of flying. During the two days he was waiting for paperwork to get him into Canada, Marvin had also been trying to talk the Customs office in Tok into letting him land there to clear Customs and save that trip to Northway. But they hung tough. No way would a Customs office, set up to deal with cars, take care of an airplane. So Marvin and the two Sisters came into Tok by way of Northway.

A rare moment in the life of a busy bush pilot.

One more member of the Warbelow family, Pepper, with a
new harness and cart.

Marvin Warbelow managing his Super Cub in the Tanana River.

Alaskan airfields aren't always glamorous: many are a bit bumpy.

The world's longest runway. Marvin Warbelow was famous for landing his airplane on the Alaska Highway.

Leaving tracks on first snow.

The Warbelow hunting camp at Joseph. Hunter is glassing for moose
from platform between trees. Courtesy of Bob Stonoff.

Bob Stonoff with beautiful wolf hide. Courtesy of Bob Stonoff.

Marvin Warbelow lands at Joseph to drop off supplies and pick up game trophies. Courtesy of Bob Stonoff.

Glassing for moose at Joseph. Courtesy of Bob Stonoff.

Moose usually don't fall next to the boat or plane and must be packed considerable distances for transport.

Roger Norris heads into the high country with Marvin Warbelow. Courtesy of Roger Norris.

Roger Norris, lower left, glassing the high country near a glacier. Courtesy of Roger Norris.

There were trophy Dall rams everywhere. Courtesy of Roger Norris.

Roger Norris picked the finest ram in sight. Courtesy of Roger Norris.

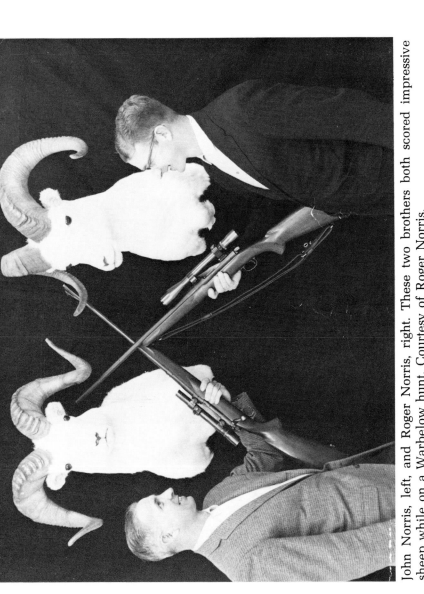

John Norris, left, and Roger Norris, right. These two brothers both scored impressive sheep while on a Warbelow hunt. Courtesy of Roger Norris.

A small band of caribou.

CHAPTER XII

Ray Mathews had come into the country some time during our years at Cathedral Bluffs. He trapped, homesteaded, mined, fished in Southeastern Alaska, guided, worked on the North Slope, and always managed to have by one means or another, an airplane. He was an excellent pilot. Just under six feet, wiry, and thin.

Every year Ray Mathews came up with something new. During hunting season of 1960, it was his swamp buggy.

Early in September, two fellows from Minneapolis stopped in to talk to Marvin about a hunting trip. We already had a lot of prospective hunters leaning over coffee cups at the counter, and Marvin was being hard put to talk to the two newcomers. When he got called to the phone, they gave up on him and left.

They went on up to Black Rapids, and there they met Ray and his stepson, Ben. They were looking for a hunt, and Ray was looking for hunters so on the spot he bought a guide's license, and for a price they agreed on, he would take them up into the Robertson River country for sheep, bear, or moose.

The four made camp twelve miles up river near the spot where years before, the river channel had been diverted, just below the glacier. The location was in virgin territory with spruce trees a foot in diameter, and the ground carpeted with lush moss twelve to fifteen inches deep. A country it seemed that hadn't been disturbed by man for at least a century.

They got in two days of hunting, but didn't find any sheep. Ben and his hunter spotted a moose, but for some reason Ben couldn't understand, the fellow wouldn't shoot it.

Then came a flash flood downstream during the night. They woke at the sound of one loud crash when the flood waters broke through a dam of boulders built up by the river itself. The men climbed trees in almost total darkness, just in time for crashing boulders and torrents of water to take the ground out from under them.

In a few minutes the water receded. They climbed down from their trees just in time for another deafening crash. This time the flood plunged across the ridge between the new and old channels, sweeping down on them like a tidal wave. They took to the trees again, and when they saw the roots washed clear of soil, feared for their lives. But once again the water receded, taking with it the foot of moss, smaller trees, and boulders. The entire landscape, static for a hundred years, was transformed in a matter of minutes.

The men managed to dig up most of their camping gear buried in silt, and knew they had to sit it out until the water went down. Eventually they ran out of food, but the river was still too high for them to travel in the swamp buggy. So Ray, a seasoned woodsman and overland hiker, left Ben with their two hunters and walked out to get help.

At flood time, tributaries become full-fledged rivers, and Ray found it impossible to cross them. He had to follow each tributary upstream until he could find a place to cross. Eventually the water would be low enough for wading, and at one point he was able to cross on a beaver dam. By the time he reached the highway, he estimated he had walked at least forty miles.

He came on down to Cathedral Bluffs and bargained with Marvin to fly him back upriver with food. But Marvin didn't figure he could land the Cessna 170 there, so promised only that he would drop food. They packed the groceries in bags ready to drop; but when they reached the campsite, the three men had done a good job of clearing out a landing strip, so they set down. Then of course, the fellows didn't want the plane to leave without them. But Marvin had just finished damaging one plane and wasn't interested in taking any more chances. He left all four of them standing on the bar, but promised that if they weren't out within a few days he would come by and drop more food to them.

"I don't expect I'll have to go back in there again," he told me on his return home. "I've seen Ray in operation too many times, and I've never seen him give up on anything yet, once he puts his mind to it He'll figure out a way to get out on his own power."

His prediction was right. The water went down, and three days later they made it back to the highway in the swamp buggy. From there they hooked a ride the ten miles down the road to Cathedral Bluffs. Ben went on to Tok and the other three settled into the one booth we had at the cafe and I fixed hamburgers and coffee for them. I had seen a lot of bedraggled and bewhiskered hunters come in from the hills, but nothing that had ever looked like they did.

They went into a huddle of long, low conversation. Several cups of coffee later, Ray slid out of the booth and left, with the understanding that his two men would stop in Tok to pay for their hunt. The disillusioned hunters sat for a while longer, lamenting the fact that time had run out for them and they still had no sheep.

"Don't feel bad about it," I advised them. "Lots of guys go home without sheep. But in the long run, you'll have a better story to tell when you get home than most fellows do." They decided maybe I was right.

CHAPTER XIII

79 Delta had been sitting on the hourglass lake all winter, and by February of 1961, we knew we couldn't procrastinate any longer. We had to get it home and back to work.

Before he had a chance to talk to the fellows from Tetlin about the job, Marvin began to think about Bob Wadsworth. Bob and his parents had come up from Montana and taken over Riverside Lodge. Bob was just 18, but a big husky fellow with poor eyesight, a booming voice, infectious laugh, and a mountain of energy. He ate like a threshing crew. He had a good team of dogs and had been freighting groceries into Tetlin all winter, so the dogs were in fine shape. Bob jumped at the chance to bring the wings out for thirty-five dollars.

He came up to Cathedral on a Friday morning so they could get an early start Saturday.

"One day should do the job," Marvin assured him.

Saturday morning they loaded Bob's team into the back of the plane and flew to the hourglass lake. They had planned that Bob could hook on to the sleds and start down the trail while Marvin hopped from lake to lake, tied down the plane each time, and back-tracked on foot to help Bob through the rough places. This worked all right except that they encountered more brush than they had planned on and had to spend time clearing out a wider trail. Then in spots the snow was deep enough so Marvin had to break trail with his snowshoes.

As a result, by Saturday night they were only halfway home. They loaded the dogs into the plane again and came home for the night.

Sunday weather was socked in tight, so it was Monday before they could finish their job. Marvin finally had to desert Bob in order to get the plane home while he could still see. So Bob fought the last four miles by himself, and finally at seven-thirty that night reached Tanacross. He was so tired by that time that he spent the night with us and went home Tuesday morning.

That four miles after dark proved to be confusing for him because he was in strange country and there were several side trails where the local Tanacross people had been cutting firewood. Marvin warned him before he took off with the plane that those trails were there, but he should just keep bearing to the left. Bob followed instructions and didn't get lost, but I think it made quite an impression on him. He slept on the davenport in the living room that night and I could hear him talking in his sleep. "Jabber, jabber...the trail....jabber...jabber. The trail divides....jabber.... jabber."

He must have had a good time, though, because he wanted to be sure he would have the job of hauling the wings back to the plane when Marvin got them rebuilt.

"I got the trail swamped out now and my dogs know the way. I might's well take them back and make another thirty-five bucks," he told us.

Corky stopped with his fuel truck a few days later enroute back to Delta where he and his folks had bought a hotel and bulk fuel service.

"I just dumped a load of fuel at Riverside," he said, "and Bob is sure wound up. I think that trip up there after them skis has been the high spot in his whole winter."

By mid-March nothing more had been done. We had dropped the plan to rebuild the wings in time to fly it out. The Colonel at Fort Greely said he would send a big cargo chopper down to lift the plane out, but that plan got scratched too. They had hauled a jeep in the chopper at one time, but thought maybe a plane's fuselage wasn't the right shape to fit in. So Bob and Marvin decided they would just go right on with their sledding operation.

Marvin intended to lash the two homemade sleds together and

load the fuselage on that, but it didn't work. The sleds were too narrow and his load top-heavy, so he finally rigged up the airplane skis with a bar welded between them and loaded the plane on top of them.

Bob's five dogs handled the sleds with floats on them with no problem, and they made that trip in one day. But the fuselage was too heavy for them. We began scouring the country for more dogs and another man. Finally a friend said he would come down the next morning with his four dogs.

With nine dogs, three men, and a lot of gear to be transported, it took three flights to the hourglass lake before they could even start operations.

"Well, at least we won't be hauling all these dogs back in the plane," Marvin told us. "We'll just feed them wherever we stop for the night and tie them up there. They can get back here on their own power."

They had hoped to be able to bring the motor from 79 Delta out by air, but we had had several days of warm weather and the snow was soft and sticky. 4404 Bravo couldn't get off with a load that heavy. This meant lashing the motor onto one of the sleds and dog-teaming it two miles to the next lake where they had room enough for a take-off. But they had barely started down the trail when Bob began to have severe stomach pains, and then passed out. He rallied, vomited, and felt better.

"I'll be all right now," Bob insisted. "I ate an orange, peeling and all on the way up here this morning from Riverside. That's probably what gave me all those stomach pains."

"I sure don't want you to pass out on me again," Marvin warned him. "I don't know what I'd do with a hundred eighty-five pounds of you if I had to carry you some place. I think I'd better take you back to Cathedral while you can still get to the plane on your own feet."

They left the help with the dogs, sled, and motor, to make what progress he could by himself, and Marvin and Bob walked down the trail to the plane.

By the time they got themselves that two miles on a soft trail and buckled in ready for take-off, Marvin decided the day was too far gone to do anything more. Before he could get Bob to Cathedral, fly back to his lake, and walk up the trail to meet the help, it would be dark.

So he wrote a note instructing the help to leave the sled where it was, and walk his dogs to the lake to be tied for the night. Marvin would bring back food for the dogs, and pick him up.

"Bob," he asked, "can you find anything back of you there to weight this note down with?"

Bob turned as far in his seat as he could and searched the back of the plane.

"Can't see nuthin' but this can of sardines."

"That's okay. All we need is a little weight."

They circled to drop the note and circled again to be sure the help got it. But when Marvin made a trip back to pick him up, he was still sitting right in the spot where they had left him. He had a cozy fire going and was warming his hands.

Marvin landed, put on his snowshoes, and tramped back that two miles on the trail. The help was still warming his hands and hadn't moved an inch since they left him there.

Marvin was furious. "What's the matter, can't you read?"

"Oh, was there a note with those sardines?" the man exclaimed.

Back at Cathedral Bluffs we weren't faring much better. As soon as Marvin had unloaded Bob and returned to the lake, we stretched our sick man out on the davenport in the living room with orders to stay quiet.

A half hour later a whole caravan of vehicles pulled into the yard. A flatbed truck piled high with mining equipment, a jeep of some sort loaded with more gear, and still a third car hauling a small trailer, filled the whole yard. Three fellows in heavy boots and work clothes, including one with a full-blown beard dyed red swarmed into the living room. They had just come up the highway from the lower states, were aiming to move into some mining property up beyond Eagle, and wanted information on having air support.

Bob was always an endless source of information on just about any subject, so while they were hashing over the pros and cons of mining in the Fortymile country, I put on a pot of coffee.

The conversation was still rolling at a lively pace when without any warning, the front door opened a few inches. The tallest, skinniest young man we had ever seen in our lives pushed his head inside, and looking directly at me, said, "I wonder if you can give me some help."

I thought it a little strange that with a whole roomful of men, he should single me out.

"Help you with what?" I asked.

"I think I have a man pinned under the car!"

In one bound, we were all on our feet and out the door - the three miners, our four little Warbelows, and I. Bob instantly forgot he was supposed to be sick, and was right behind us at the end of the line.

Sure enough, right across the highway from our gas pumps, was a yellow pickup truck lying on its side in the ditch, with the driver's door up.

Before we ever got across the yard and on to the road, a head appeared, coming out through the rolled-down window, and out crawled the second tallest, skinniest young man we had ever seen. He was plowing his way through a whole case of bread that had been sitting on the seat between them when they tipped. Several bottles of good whiskey, tucked in among the loaves of bread to keep them from breaking, were falling all over the floor.

The driver, assuming that his passenger had been thrown under the car, didn't realize until now that he had simply been buried in bread and whiskey. He was so relieved that they took time out to let us know that each one was six feet, four inches tall.

The boys were from the Alaska Communications System station in Tok and were on their way home from the commissary in Delta when they lost control of the car. They were both concerned about what their commanding officer was going to say about this situation, so we decided the sooner they got the car back on its wheels, the better. Bob had a rope in the back of his truck. So with that tied to the jeep, and with all hands lifting on the underside of the pickup, they pulled it out of the ditch and sent the two fellows on their way home.

Marvin and the help flew in from the lake a bit later but the help didn't stick with the job any longer. That night he decided he had to go home for a dry pair of socks. And as soon as he got home he phoned Marvin.

"I'm not going back up there," he announced. "Have my dogs at your place for me at nine o'clock tomorrow morning."

"What do ya mean, have your dogs here at nine!" Marvin stormed. "I said when I took those dogs up there they'd come out on their own power, and by gosh that's the way they're going to come!"

"Then I'll be up there to get them myself!" And by mutual consent they both hung up.

"He'll never get there tomorrow morning," Bob insisted. "Let's get up early and get as much work out of them dogs as we can before he picks them up."

But Bob hadn't figured all the angles. He and Marvin started early, but the help didn't come down get his own dogs. He called his brother, and by mid-morning, that man was up the trail to meet them.

Bob Felch from Tok heard about our dilemma, so he came up with four of his own dogs and spent the last few days helping the fellows finish the job. They could never have done it without him.

The fuselage was a lot wider than the wings and pontoons, so the men literally had to blaze a trail eight feet wide all the way from the hourglass lake to Tanacross, and they spent days doing it.

"There was one time when I sat down with my machete and whacked down fifteen trees without even moving," Bob Wadsworth declared.

By the time we finally got everything in one pile at Cathedral Bluffs, Art Smith had the wings rebuilt, and 79 Delta was once again in the air.

CHAPTER XIV

About 1959, the federal government began to build a string of towers that stretched from Point Barrow down to Colorado Springs. Operational headdquarters for those towers in the area from Fairbanks south was at Clear. There they had the big radar screens that looked out over the top of the world. These towers, spaced twenty miles apart, were labeled the BMEWS-Balistic Missile Early Warning System. The "A" segment went down to the coast toward Valdez, and the "B" section parallelled the Alaska Highway. They were equipped to pass rapidly down the continent any danger signals of enemy aircraft entering American zones.

Western Electric installed the motors and all the radio gear housed in the shops built at the base of each tower. By 1961, their work was done, and Federal Electric was given the contract to maintain both the motors and electrical system. This required not only mechanics, but radio technicians as well.

A few of these towers were built far enough off the highway so they could be reached only by air. Such was the tower at Gold King Creek, about an hour's flight back off the highway from Delta toward Fairbanks.

Chuck Meuli who was in charge of the operations in our area, came down to see us one day.

"We've got to make regular trips from Delta out to Gold King twice a week," he said. "There's no air service based in Delta, so we're either going to have to bring a plane out from Fairbanks each time, or strike up a deal with you. Distance-wise, it's a toss-up. Both places are about a hundred miles away from us. It's going to be a matter of where we can get the best deal."

"What's involved?" Marvin wanted to know.

"We need to take one to three men out each trip and have you stand by for them while they do their routine maintenance work."

This meant dead runs between Cathedral Bluffs and Delta, but we couldn't turn it down. Marvin started those flights in February of 1961 and ten years later we were still flying them.

That first year, they had endless problems with their motors. In addition to the two routine trips, there were always emergency trips in the middle of the night, in bad weather, or on holidays in order to keep the machinery going. More than once the men ended up spending the night out there and sleeping in their bags on benches. The landing strip sat up on a rise above the tower base, barely long enough for take-off with unfavorable winds or sticky snow. And because both ends of the strip dropped off into nothingness, there was no way to lengthen it.

Every fall the crew had to spend several days out there doing a major overhaul on all the motors. Although Marvin started prodding them weeks ahead of time every year, they never managed to get it done until December when flying conditions were the worst. One year, they didn't get out there until three days before Christmas. Their last words to Marvin when he left were, "Be sure you don't leave us here over Christmas!"

As might be expected, the weather fouled up. The day before Christmas it hadn't improved, but he felt he had to get them out. As soon as we had enough daylight for take-off, he started out intending to go directly to Gold King and bypass Delta. An hour later I had a call from the RCA office in Tok.

"We just had a call from our Delta office. They're in contact with Gold King and said to tell Marv not to come out. It's zero-zero out there. They can't even see the field from the shop."

"Marvin left an hour ago, I told him. "Isn't there some way you can stop him?"

The Delta FAA station tried to call him, but either he didn't have his radio on or reception was poor. They never contacted him.

That was a miserable Christmas Eve for the four children and me. Late that night I had another cal from the RCA office in Tok to tell me that the plane got down at Gold King, but it might be a long time before they could get out of there again. Fortunately, weather improved Christmas morning, and about noon our plane and pilot were back home again.

The Tetlin mail run was increased to twice-a-week deliveries. With three scheduled flights a week, we had a rough time wedging other flights in-between. It seemed they were continually interfering with the schedule or vice versa.

Take-off for Gold King had to be at 7 A.M. in order to pick up a crew in Delta by eight. One July evening just as Marvin went to bed, he remarked, "I have the plane all gassed up tonight so I can sleep in 'til the last minute tomorrow morning."

About midnight, we got a call from the Health Department in Fairbanks wanting the plane to pick up a man in Tetlin and fly into town. They'd had a report that he was in critical condition with a nosebleed.

The man was on his feet when Marvin landed in Tetlin, and didn't seem nearly as sick as the lady in Fairbanks thought he was. But they flew into town anyway.

Marvin knew he could never get back to Cathedral Bluffs in time that night to get any sleep before he had to start out for Delta again in the morning, so he just stopped at Delta on his way back from Fairbanks, curled up in the plane, and waited until eight o'clock for his crew to go to Gold King.

About fifteen minutes after he left home for the hospital that night, two men came pounding on the door. They were in a real tizzy and wanted a flight up to Joe's Village immediately. Joe's Village, more properly called Joseph, was a hundred miles or more back in the hills toward Eagle. The fellows had recently located something up there they believed was a valuable mineral, but they hadn't been able to get back there to stake claims. That evening they had just heard that some men from Fairbanks were going to Joseph in a chopper, and they were in a panic for fear someone else had a lead and would get their spot staked before they could.

"But Marvin isn't going to be able to take you up there until tomorrow afternoon when he gets home from Gold King."

"Then we'll sit right here and wait for him," one man declared.

They went down to the bunkhouse, rolled out their sleeping bags, and stayed the night. They paced the floor of the cafe all the next morning, and finally early that afternoon, Marvin showed. The two were at the plane before he could crawl out.

"What's up guys?" Marvin asked. With these two, he knew he could expect anything.

"We've got to get up to Joe's just as soon as we can, Marv!" one told him.

Marvin about wilted. "Good gosh, I haven't had a wink of sleep since night before last. I sat in this darned plane all last night at Delta and I've had it. What's the big hurry, anyway?"

They both squirmed a bit. "Well," the other mumbled, "we can't exactly tell you. Sort of secretive, you know."

"Okay. Okay, I know. Found another gold mine, I suppose. But I'll have to have a little sleep first."

They paced the floor for another two hours while Marvin got his cat nap. Then he loaded up their gear and they were off for Joseph.

The Joseph strip was a bad one. He could get down with his load, but knew he could never get off with it again. So the fellows took our machete along and while they were there they cut a swath of weeds and buckbrush a thousand feet long and wide enough for the plane to set down in. With the two days they had allotted for their stay there, plus a few more while Marvin waited for a spell of foul weather to pass, they had plenty of time to clear the strip.

A week later Marvin was called out again, this time at three-thirty in the morning, to pick up a technician at Delta and take him into Gold King. This time they had radio problems. He didn't get back home until nine-thirty that morning. We had two sheep hunters who had been sitting here for three days waiting for weather to clear up in the hills, but they finally gave up and went home without ever making it into sheep country. Sheep season had been shoved up ten days that year to avoid the rainy season that sets in about August 20, but all that happened was that the rain moved up ten days, too.

Those trips to Gold King became almost rituals. We were both up, never later than six o'clock. While I packed a lunch and cooked his breakfast, Marvin got into his greasy clothes and went out to firepot. Once the engine was warmed up, he'd start it up for a few minutes, turn it off, cover the nose with a heavy canvas, and come in to change clothes and have breakfast. Then came ten to fifteen minutes that were priceless to both of us. We'd sit down in our chairs in the living room and talk. Sometimes that was the only ten or fifteen minutes we'd have to ourselves all day, because by the time he came home at night, the lodge would be full of people.

I always went to the airstrip with him. During the winter months, we had the last minute job of rubbing snow off the wings. Then we would unknot the tiedowns on the struts and tail wheel. Marvin would hand me the electric heater we kept in the cabin until the last minute, and crawl into the plane. I'd walk beside him while he taxied to the end of the strip. Just before revving up for take-off, he'd open the door and call out, "See you later, alligator!" and roll down the runway.

No matter what the family stresses had been the day before or up until this moment, I had strong feelings about never wanting him to leave with any ill feelings between us, and he must have felt the same. I'd wave goodbye, whisper a simple prayer to myself, "Please, God, make it safe," and hold my breath until the plane had lifted safely off the end of the strip, and cleared the trees at the bottom of the hill. Even then I'd stand and watch until it steadily shrunk in size to a miniature, and then a speck, and finally became a part of the sky.

Those trees at the lower edge of the strip were a constant hazard, especially six or eight of the taller ones.

"Marvin, why don't we cut those tall trees down there?" I'd ask him, and he would always come up with the same answer.

"They aren't on our land. They belong to the state, and we can't cut them."

"Better we cut the state's trees than crash an airplane," I'd argue. But the trees remained.

Ron and I finally took care of that. One morning after the plane left, we took the crosscut saw down to the woods and downed them all. I was amazed at the power of that saw because neither Ron nor I had ever used one before. Those trees were big, and every time one of them fell, Ron boomed out, "Timber!"

Several days passed before Marvin realized his hazards were gone. It was too late to do anything about it and I think he was relieved that the job was done. Besides, I don't think the state really cared.

CHAPTER XV

Helen Foster made quite an impact on our lives. A short little lady just turned forty, she was a senior geologist with the Alaska branch of the U.S. Geological Survey. Although they head-quartered in Menlo Park, California, Helen and her crew of geologists and assistants spent every summer in Alaska. Helen concentrated on the vast area known as the 40-Mile country; and beginning in 1960, spent every season for the next ten years at Cathedral Bluffs.

She chose Cathedral for several reasons. We lived in sort of an informal hodgepodge, and since her crews varied from two or three people to as many as ten, that suited her purpose well. Helen herself was allergic to a lot of food, mainly onions and spices, and I was one of the few cooks along the highway who would cater to her tastes. But most importantly, they needed the use of an airplane. We had two, and in later years, three and four planes at her disposal.

She had spent the ten years of occupation right after the close of World War II in Japan. Her stories were fascinating. The kids adored her, and she came close to making geologists out of all of them. They went with her on rock-hunting trips, and at night helped her and her assistant sort and sack them. They had rock collections of their own so big they had to build a shack to house them in one summer.

Part of the work the geologists did was along the road, so they could drive a car up the Taylor Highway, park it somewhere, and walk in for several days at a time. But otherwise, Marvin flew them into their spots. Helen's assistants were usually young women who were doing graduate work toward a Master's degree. They had to be tough, because she was. Those two girls would climb into the plane with everything they needed for a trip of anywhere from two days to two weeks packed on their backs. Marvin would drop them off on a ridge somewhere up in the 40-Mile, and at the end of their designated time, pick them up on another ridge miles away from the first one. They'd come home with canvas bags of rocks, tired and hungry, ready for a hamburger and a shower.

Since we moved out of our house every spring and into the lodge that we operated only during the summer months, the geologists usually took over the house. Some of the men who had families brought them up from California for the summer and moved into one of our little house trailers scattered around the place, or set up their own tents. They were down-to-earth people, and our youngsters had plenty of playmates every summer.

The geologists very soon learned to adjust to the unpredictable schedules of the airplanes. If they were all packed ready to fly when an emergency came up, they were quite willing to wait their turn. Sometimes they had to wait at the other end, too.

That summer of 1960, Helen and her assistant, Mona, had been out for several days and were scheduled to be picked up before dark on their last day. Marvin was just firing up the 170 to go find them when we got a call from Dot Lake.

"We've got a boy up here who drank poison at a teen-age party and he's in convulsions," the frightened voice told him. "We've got to get him to Fairbanks!"

"If he's in convulsions, I can't take him without someone going along," Marvin reminded her.

There were no Emergency Medical Technicians in the country in 1960, so when Marvin landed at Dot Lake, a man was ready to go along with the patient.

Helen and Mona sat on their ridge and waited until after dark before Marvin got back from Fairbanks to pick them up.

Hunting season always brought its own peculiar brand of problems. That year it was Ritch.

Ritch had come up from San Francisco and, the day before season opened, stopped in on his way south. He had just spent three months at Eielson Air Force Base outside of Fairbanks installing a liquor bar. His job was not only to design and help build it, but then he had to stay around long enough to watch it in operation and determine whether or not the design had to be changed. "Efficiency expert" he was called.

He had a few days to spare and was interested in a moose hunting trip.

"I don't want any meat," he told Marvin. "Just the horns."

"It's illegal to shoot an animal and not salvage all the usable meat, you know. I don't take out fellows who intend to break the law. In fact, I wouldn't dare do it even if I wanted to. I could lose my pilot's license."

"Well, I'm willing to bring the meat out. But can't I just give it away to someone?"

We always needed a moose for ourselves every fall, but it was usually one of the last days of season before flying slowed up enough for Marvin to get out and look for one.

"Tell you what I'll do, Ritch. I'll take you out and you pay for the round trip. You get the horns and I'll take the meat. That way it won't cost you anything to get the meat flown out."

Ritch was happy with that.

"But just remember one thing," Marvin added. "There's a lot of meat on a moose and I don't intend to pack it a mile. I'll be taking you in with the float plane onto a lake just a few miles from here. You will either have to shoot your animal right at the lake or else pack it there so I can load it into the plane."

That, too, was all right with Ritch. So he settled in at the cafe to wait until Marvin had time to get him out.

John Bartholomew was the Presbyterian missionary at Tok, and our two families were close friends. John was a brilliant young man, had a keen sense of humor, and love to fly. He and his minister friend from Delta, also named John, were coming up later that day to be flown in for a moose hunt, too.

Marvin warned Ritch, "Now we've got these two ministers

coming up this afternoon, and I know they wouldn't think too kindly of your bar-building profession, so it might be better if you just don't mention it to them."

Ritch was an extremely pleasant person. For the third time that day he agreed.

The Ministers arrived, sat down in the booth opposite Ritch, and the conversation shortly turned to Ritch's reason for being there.

"Up here visiting?" John Bartholomew wanted to know.

"No. Marv is taking me out for a moose," Ritch explained casually.

"Did you drive up the highway?"

"Yes."

"How's the road?"

"Well, I don't know how it is right now," Ritch admitted. "I came up about three months ago. It was in fair shape then."

"You've been here three months? What did you do all that time?" The other John wanted to know.

I could see Ritch's foot wiggling back and forth under the table, and knew he was already squirming.

"Well, I was doing some carpentering out at Eielson Air Base."

"Yes? And what kind of carpentering?"

"Oh, just routine work."

At this point the first John realized Ritch was growing uncomfortable and diplomatically tried to change the subject. But the other John persisted.

"Well, what do you mean by routine work? You must have been doing something specific."

Ritch gave me a short, uneasy glance, then turned back to his inquisitor.

"I'm an efficiency expert."

"Efficiency expert!" exclaimed the other John. "Efficiency expert at what?"

132

Ritch had reached the end of his rope.

"Well, to tell the truth, I was there designing and building a bar. Then I had to stay long enough to watch it in operation. If there had been anything wrong with the design, I would have changed it. That's what an efficiency expert does."

The other John shook his head. "Why on earth," he asked, with deep emphasis on every word, "would anyone want to make a bar more efficient?"

Ritch, by this time, was purple. "So you can get them drunk just that much faster and get them off the stools to make room for the next ones!"

The other John was stunned for a minute, but he wasn't satisfied. "I still wonder," he continued, "why you ever chose a profession like that?"

"Well," Ritch drawled, "I'm too lazy to work and I'm afraid to steal!"

So, with all that cleared up, they changed the subject.

Ritch didn't follow instructions too well. He shot his moose a half mile away from the lake, with nothing but dense underbrush all the way. The moose was huge, and he decided that with a trophy of that size, he wanted the whole head, horns and all. So, in spite of everything Marvin had told him about getting the meat out first and the horns last, he started for the lake dragging head and horns behind him. In short order, he stumbled over a log and wrenched his back so bad he had to leave his loot and hobble to the lake. When Marvin flew over that evening to check on him, there sat Ritch waiting for him. Marvin landed to see what was wrong.

"You know, Marv," he added at the end of his story, "those eyes just kept looking up at me, and when I hurt my back, I thought, 'Now maybe this is just his way of getting even with me.'"

Marvin brought him back to Cathedral Bluffs where he decided he would have to hire someone else to pack out his moose meat and head. It was obvious that Ritch was not only crippled up, but he was spooked.

While we were phoning around the country looking for someone to rescue the meat, a young couple from California came through in a jeep on their way up to Fairbanks to go to the University. Ritch offered them thirty dollars to bring out his moose. They needed the money, so agreed to do it.

Marvin flew them into his lake and walked them back to the moose so they'd know where it was before he left them. He packed one load of the meat out himself on their return trip, and brought those three pieces home with him. But then the kids got lost and couldn't find the moose the second time. Although the wife was faring pretty well, the husband had fallen and twisted his back and had blisters all over his feet. When Marvin stopped in a day later, they had just been milling around in a circle and still hadn't located their meat, so they wanted to get out. They were fed up.

So was Marvin. "Look," he told them, "we made a bargain. I'm hauling you in and out of here free to get this job done, I'm not hauling in anyone else. Besides, that meat is probably spoiling already. I'll go back with you once more and we'll mark the trail with orange tape so you won't get lost again. I'm on my way up further to pick up the two ministers before dark. I'll be back after you in the morning."

He marked their trail, they each packed out another load of meat, and he left them to finish the job.

It poured rain all that night and most of the next day. By the time Marvin got in to pick them up the following morning, they were standing on the lake shore waving a distress signal.

"We thought you'd forgotten us! Thought we were deserted!" they wailed.

"You didn't expect me to come in with all that rain, did you?" asked Marvin. Then he noted that they had cut the legs off their jeans and were standing there soaking wet, barefooted, and shivering in shorts.

"What on earth happened to your pants?" he wanted to know.

"We were soaked!" explained the girl. "That rain just poured through our tent all night and our jeans were dripping. We had to cut the legs off with a jackknife and hang them out to dry." Sure enough, the four legs were draped over a clump of bush

134

nearby.

Marvin got his passengers back to Cathedral Bluffs, their teeth still chattering with the cold. While I got them into a hot tub of water to warm them up, he went back to pick up the rest of the meat himself.

"Too bad you wrecked those jeans," I remarked.

"Oh, we didn't wreck them," the wife assured me. "I brought the legs along so we can sew them back on."

Ritch, an experienced butcher, stayed on a couple of days to help us take care of our meat. His head and horns didn't make it. Marvin took a look at them on his last trip to the lake, but a porcupine had already found them and the horns were badly chewed. They were still sitting beside the stump where Ritch dropped them when he packed his gear and headed south.

CHAPTER XVI

By November, we knew we could never accomplish that Gold King winter flying with a 170. There just weren't enough horses to do the job. So we made a deal with Bob Mifflin in Spokane to trade one of the two planes in on a Cessna 180. He offered us a five thousand dollar trade-in on Bravo. One of his pilots would fly the new plane up for us and take Bravo back. Bob said he would pay the pilot's salary if we paid his expenses. That was a good deal all around.

"We'd better get Art Smith down here to work on both these airplanes," Marvin decided. "It's easier to get him to come down here than for me to take two planes up there. 79 Delta needs a hundred-hour, and Mifflin wants a periodic on Bravo before his man picks it up."

Art came down to Cathedral Bluffs, but the weather was miserable. We were having snow storms, sleet, and cold winds. With no shop to work in, the men were half frozen. In order to drain the fuel lines, they draped motor covers over the wings and set up a fire pot inside to thaw out any ice build-up there might be. For two days, November 14 and 15, Marvin and Art worked almost non-stop. By the end of the second day they were all finished except for some work on the fuselage of 79 Delta. They had the tail feathers off, but since Art had converted an army surplus quonset hut into a small shop at home, he decided it would be easier to take the tail pieces up to Big Delta with him and work on them there. We had our wheel skis mounted on Bravo and the conventional skis on Delta, so there was no great hurry about the tail feathers. Delta was only a stand-by.

November 16 was my sister's birthday. I always think of birthdays as being good omens, so I didn't mind getting up early that morning. It was destined to be a good day.

Cathedral Bluffs sits so close into the foot of the Alaska Range, that from mid-November until the first week in February, we never saw the sun. We had some long, dark winters up there.

That morning, as usual, we fire-potted the plane, covered the motor, and then went into the house for our few minutes of waiting for a seven o'clock take-off. Although Marvin was using the strip that morning, he could gain an extra hundred feet of runway if he swung out onto the highway from our driveway, and then made a gentle right-hand swerve onto the strip. Ron was up and dressed, so he walked back down the road a couple of blocks to watch for any early morning driver who might be coming from the Tok direction. I stayed at the upper end of the strip for my usual goodbye.

Marvin taxied up the driveway and made his right-hand turn onto the road, checked both magnetos, and the plane revved up nicely. The landing light came on, bright in the blackness of the morning, and sent a long beam down the road, and then onto the field as the plane moved on down the strip. At the lower end the wheels hit the bump, and Bravo bounced into the air. I couldn't even see the outline of the plane, just the tiny flicks of the position lights and landing light, and then the landing light went off. The hum of the motor and the two tiny flicks were all that were left.

Then something happened. The motor began to spit. Marvin was losing power, and then altitude. He wasn't more than two hundred feet in the air, and he knew he was going down. To his left was the highway-a good, safe landing place. But he didn't dare make too sharp a turn and stall out. He tried a gradual turn, but Bravo was settling in fast, like a dead duck. He was within twenty feet of the road, and still floating, when a tree loomed up just ahead of him, between him and the road. To turn in either direction meant stalling, and to go straight ahead meant cutting his left wing in two with the tree trunk. He chose the tree.

From the upper end of the strip I could see the landing lights settling, and then disappear below the tree tops. There was one loud thud, and then silence.

"Ron!" I screamed into the darkness behind me, "Your Dad went down!"

Ron came running down the road. "Where?" he kept asking. "Where?"

"Just across the river, right around the first bend. He must have landed on the road, but I heard the click, so I know it was a hard landing!"

We both ran top speed down the hill that parallelled the airstrip, and across the first little bridge. But when we reached the first turn, there was nothing. We kept on running, puffing hard, and our hearts banging against our ribs. Around the second turn we still saw and heard nothing. But then we began to see the blurred outline of something moving toward us.

We stopped to catch our breath. "How bad is it?" I called.

"I don't know," came Marvin's disgusted answer. "I just walked out through the hole where the door used to be, and didn't even look back."

Together we walked in silence back to the crash site, and Ron and I were horrified when we realized the plane wasn't on the road at all. It was wound around a birch tree twenty feet off the edge of the road. Damage was great.

"The wing clipped the top right off that tree," Marvin lamented. "There was no way around it."

We walked the half mile back to the house to make phone calls to RCA and to Art Smith, then sat down to plan our line of attack.

Lavell Wilson and Bert Thompson, stationed at Dot Lake to maintain the RCA site near there, came right down to help Marvin take the wings off Bravo and haul it back home. They worked fast, but in spite of them we had quite a gathering of sightseers. The door on the pilot's side of the fuselage had popped right off its hinges and flown into the brush. Along with it went the log books and everything loose, including a carton of Baby Ruth candy bars. People went crazy scrounging around in the muck and snow and slush and brush looking for those candy bars, but no one offered to return them.

Art Smith came right down that same day with the tail feathers in hand, and spent another two days getting 79 Delta back in the air. Since his family had gone stateside for the winter, and their Shetland pony, Pepper, had moved in with us, we had invited Art down for Thanksgiving dinner. But after two trips to Cathedral within a week, he didn't think he would want to make a third one that month. So when he came down the morning of the sixteenth, he brought a turkey with him.

"At the rate we're both going," he explained to Marvin, "neither of us will last until Thanksgiving, and I want to be sure I get my turkey."

So I cooked two Thanksgiving dinners that month, although at the time I didn't think I had much to be thankful for.

A post-mortem of Bravo proved that it still had some ice in the fuel lines.

"If we'd had that thing in a hangar when we did the hundred-hour, this wouldn't have happened," Marvin concluded, and Art agreed. But neither of them had a hangar big enough for a plane.

Now we needed that 180 more than ever, but our five thousand dollar down payment wasn't there any more. We had to do some scraping to come up with the cash.

There was some delay before Mifflin could get the plane underway from Spokane, and then we got bogged down with long stretches of bitterly cold weather. So it was mid-December before 36 Tango finally went to work for us. Miraculously, the wheel skis that had gone through the crash at the birch tree survived with no damage, so they went to work with the new 180.

Marvin had both planes at Delta when the long, cold spell of December 1961 set in. From December 6 until New Year's night it never got warmer than minus fifty, and sometimes dipped to seventy below.

Marvin got stuck at Delta with both planes, making futile attempts to get out to the Gold King site.

The RCA site supervisor, was worried about his motors out at Gold King, so he was right on our case every day trying to get his technicians up on the hill. Marvin told him repeatedly he couldn't fly until it warmed up.

One of those mornings they had a real confrontation.

"You'd better get out to the field and start firepotting that plane," the supervisor yelled, and walked out the door of his office.

Marvin turned to the two technicians standing there. "Well, if that's what he wants, I guess we can go down there and firepot. But I can tell him we aren't going any place."

"Do you think it would be a safe operation if we did go?" Mark asked.

"No."

"Then I'm not going." Mark jumped into his car and caught up with the supervisor down the road.

"I'm not flying, even if the plane does go."

"You can either fly or get fired!" the boss shouted through the crack in his window.

But when he called his Anchorage office, they turned thumbs down on the firing, so Mark stayed on.

They finally got out to Gold King a few days later, and that should have straightened things out, but it didn't. They had 35 knot headwinds all the way back to Delta, so it was dark before they got in. Marvin had a landing light and had done a fair amount of night flying, so could have been all right if everyone had left him alone. But the supervisor saw those navigation lights three or four miles away, and panicked. He got two trucks out on the runway with their lights on. But he had them parked with their backs to the wind, so when the fellows came in, they were staring right into those four headlights. There was nothing to do but make a down-wind landing, and with a thirty-five knot tailwind on a short field, that wasn't easy.

Then they realized that one of the trucks was sitting right in the middle of the strip about a third of the way down the field. At the same time, someone standing back of the truck turned on a flashlight and started flashing it in their faces. With no brakes on his skis, Marvin took to the side of the field to avoid hitting the fellow with the flashlight, and tore up the leading edge of his wing in the brush.

They zig-zagged to a halt, and Mark jumped out of the plane. He made a few giant leaps toward the holder of the flashlight and stared his boss, in the face.

"I thought I knew all the swear words in the book," Marvin related to us later, "but I found out I didn't. Mark knew more."

In the meantime, the mail run at Tok was overdue, and getting further overdue every day. But even road traffic had come to a standstill, so the postmistress didn't put too much pressure on me. The mail truck from Fairbanks and Delta wasn't making runs, so there was no mail to go to Tetlin anyway.

We had half a ton of freight for Tetlin sitting over in the motor room, too, and with no reprieve from the weather day after day, we finally had to handsled it all to the house and store it in the middle of the living room floor to keep it from freezing.

Finally, the day before Christmas, a brave family from Tok drove all the way to Fairbanks to do Christmas shopping, and Marvin caught a ride home from Delta with them. His two planes sat at Art's shop until the morning after New Years when Lavell Wilson phoned. We were still in bed when the call came.

"Want to go to Delta today to get a plane?" he asked. "It warmed up during the night. It's way up to minus thirty-five this morning."

Marvin jumped into his clothes and was ready to go when Lavell stopped by a half hour later with the RCA truck enroute to the sites along the highway. It took him the rest of the day to warm up a plane that had been sitting for three weeks during the worst cold of the decade, but at last we had 79 Delta down at our front door again.

CHAPTER XVII

It had taken Marvin all the way from Wisconsin to the Arctic Circle to learn how to fly his first 170. Now he was up another step and had to figure out how to fly a 180. It was heavier and zippier than anything else he had ever flown.

December wasn't a good time to do his learning. We had two moose wintering there, and most of their time they spent on the airstrip. Marvin usually had to circle until someone could get out there and drive them off. The airstrip had three feet snow on it, and although the 170's could skim across the top, the heavier plane couldn't. The first half of a landing was usually all right, but about mid-strip enough speed had been dissipated so the full weight of the 180 settled down on the snow, and invariably one ski would break through. Down would go a wingtip, and we had to shovel to get the plane out of the hole and into its parking place.

Our alternative was the road beside the strip, but there were drifts ten feet high on both sides of the road that winter, and not enough room between them to clear the wingtips. Besides, we had a running battle on for years with the state trooper at Tok about those road landings, and tried to avoid it as much as possible.

The tourists, in general, enjoyed it though. After miles of wild country and potholes, it was a welcome sight to see a flagman down the road holding them up so a plane could land. It gave them a chance to get out and stretch their legs, or chat with a local sourdough for awhile.

The army held its annual winter maneuvers at the Tanacross airfield every year, so a lot of the traffic we had to stop was military. I was mortified one day when I stopped a truck, and then realized that a whole convoy was right behind it. Eight trucks all told pulled up and waited. The driver in the first truck rolled down his window.

"I'm sorry about this," I began to apologize. "I hope you don't lose the war on account of us."

"No trouble," he assured me. "We're not fighting. We're just the supply crew."

Then there was the young man from Fort Wainwright who was there one day when the plane came in. He ran outside to watch the landing, then came back into the cafe.

"Man, I've waited four years to see this!"

"See what?" I asked.

"That plane landing on the road."

"How did you know it was going to land on the road?" I wanted to know.

"Oh, gosh, everybody in Fort Wainwright knows about that guy who lands on the Alaska Highway! He's got the longest runway in the world."

That kind of publicity we didn't want, but at least we had our problems at Tok resolved. It had become impossible to land in the ditch at the road commission any longer because more and more homesteaders were settling along the highway and power lines were a hazard. So Marvin made a deal with Bob Roberts to use his pickup on mail days to haul mail back and forth from the post office. The Roberts family -- brothers Bob and Ellis, and Ellis's wife Mary -- lived right across the road from the airstrip, so all Marvin had to do was walk across the road to get the car. But then it got to the point where he didn't even want to walk across the road, so he began to taxi across the plane, park right beside the living room window, and then when he got ready for take-off, they'd get the full blast of his tailwash, snow and all, against the house.

"Why on earth do you put up with that?" I'd ask them once in awhile.

But there wasn't much going during those winter months, and

Grizzlies near the Tanana River. Courtesy of Lavell Wilson.

Wading icy steam in the high country.

Beautiful Dall ram with Carl Charles, another Warbelow hunter.

Typical mountain terrain in the Forty Mile area. Photo by Carl Charles

The sun shines around the clock during Alaska's August. This camp is set up for the convenience of one of the many Warbelow's clients. Photo by Carl Charles.

Caribou are perpetual wanderers.

Marvin Warbelow taking off on a remote lake after dropping off hunters. Photo by Carl Charles.

Good food is of utmost importance in any hunting camp as these hearty hunters certainly will attest.

Marvin Warbelow and two fat trout.

Young Beeker with bag over to ... her Dall sheep.

Two more Warbelow hunters with nice trophies.

Study group consisting of a pair of one-year-old juveniles. Photo by Dr. a. Warhol, smbile ssisviines a'Aeol' a Dessert

Griz cub gets weighed. Photo by Ron Warbelow while assisting Alaska Department of Fish and Game.

In the alpine

Lavell Wilson, left, chief pilot for 40-Mile Air, and Steve Leriget, pilot, give dog mushers and dogs a lift.

Willy Lou Warbelow with her sons' Cessna 206.

they enjoyed watching the comings and goings of freight and passengers. Besides, it precluded their ever having to hand shovel snow for banking against that side of the house.

Marvin liked it too, because Mary's coffee pot was always on, and he managed to find time betweens runs to sit at their long table and chew the fat every mail day.

"Better drink your coffee today while I can, Mary. When the temperature hits minus fifty, I'm heading for the Bahamas!"

"Hold up a minute, while I pack my bag. I'm going with you!" was Mary's stock reply.

Al Stout was usually there at the Roberts' table too, and sometimes Bill Simmons or Walt Sebulski-all old sourdoughs well-saturated with Alaskan stories, and mellowed with years of reminiscing. They were all either pilots or miners, and sometimes both.

Their hours at that table weren't wasted. They exchanged flying stories, and discussed accidents. Every experience, whether first or second hand, usually taught them something about flying safety they hadn't known before. One that intrigued them was the sonic boom gimmick. Don Sheldon had gone down somewhere over on the Yukon. Although he maintained contact with the FAA, he didn't know where he was. So the army located him with a sonic boom device. They sent a plane over the general area where Sheldon was down, and broke the sound barrier. The airborne pilot called in the instant he heard his boom, and Sheldon did likewise. With that information, they could calculate the distance between the two planes. It gave them a radius to work on, and the second time around the military crew found their man.

The fellows at the table debated the pros and cons of what kind of emergency rations to carry, and how far you could stretch your luck on adverse weather conditions. But one of the most valuable outcomes of the long talks was a gentlemen's agreement among Bob, Ellis, Bill, and Marvin that whenever one of them got into trouble, the others would start looking for him.

Over the years, more flying hours were piled up looking for Marvin than for all the rest of them put together, but Ellis had his day, too. On August 15, 1967 he flew the Family Cruiser up to Joseph and didn't come back. Bob went looking for him with the float plane and found him sitting on the Joseph field, the plane upside down about midway down the strip.

Since Bob could hardly land on floats at that time, he returned home and alerted Marvin.

"That plane is right in the middle of the strip, Marvin. I don't think you can get in there with a load at all."

"No problem. Ellis and I can flip that thing back on its wheels by ourselves," Marvin assured him.

But he was wrong. He and Ellis together couldn't budge it. So he left Ellis with the plane and went back to Tok for help. They finally decided to chance landing with a load on half a strip, and both Bob and Al Stout climbed into the plane with him. They managed the short landing, and it took all four of them to right the Cruiser. It had too much wing damage to risk flying it home, so they pushed it off the field and tied it down. This gave them enough footage to lift off with all four of them in the 180, and they came home to powwow over a cup of coffee at Mary's table about their next move. In the end, Bob and Ellis took their Cub off its floats, and with that to ferry themselves back and forth, they repaired the damage at Joseph and brought their PA14 back to home base.

Those old miners and prospectors were a hardy bunch. In March of '62, Marvin flew Paul Kirkstetter back to Joe's village to do his assessment work. He never liked taking one man in alone, and this time Skip Cady, who usually went with him didn't go. Paul planned to stay a week, but he knew there was always the possibility that Marvin couldn't get him out on schedule.

"Now do you have food enough in case I can't get you out when I'm supposed to?" Marvin asked just before they took off.

"I got bullets," Paul grinned.

We never had to worry about Paul. He really did know how to live off the land. While he was doing his assessment work every spring, he ran a wolf and wolverine trapline, and usually came out with a nice bundle of fur. One year he and Skip flew in, but then walked out all the way from Joseph, wolf-hunting along the route.

That same spring of 1962, two old miners came out from Fairbanks to fly up into the Seventymile country near Dawson. Marvin dreaded that trip because it meant landing on a poor field in a narrow canyon with two thousand foot sides, and lots of snow. He got them in safely, but didn't have to worry about getting them out. They mined all summer, then walked out to Boundary in the fall where they had a pickup truck parked.

Fred Cook and old John Hajdukovich were another pair. John had come over from Yugoslavia somewhere back in the 1800's, and settled finally at Delta. For years he ran barges on the Tanana all the way from Fairbanks to Delta and Tanacross, and even freighted into Tetlin. He had trading posts at all these places and brought in his own supplies. In more recent years he teamed up with Fred who was a much younger man, and they did a lot of prospecting together. They, too, would have Marvin fly them up into the Joseph country or over into Rumble Creek on the Robertson River, and spend two or three weeks at a time digging around in the dirt.

John was 79 the last time we flew him out. He came to Cathedral alone and wanted to go out for a week. Marvin flat said no.

"There's a limit, John. It's bad enough when you go out with Fred at your age, but no way am I going to take you out alone. You could get sick or get hurt, and it isn't worth the risk."

John was silent for a long time, then wandered around the yard for awhile. Finally, he came back inside.

"All right if you don't want to take me out. But I'm going anyway. If you won't take me, I'll walk in."

There was no way he could be talked out of it. So with a lot of misgivings, Marvin loaded him into the plane and flew him out, with specific instructions that a week later they were to meet in the same spot.

Marvin kept his appointment on time, but John didn't. When the plane landed, there was no sign of him. Marvin began tramping out in first one direction and then another, frantically calling. Finally he found him, curled up like a kitten under a tree, sound asleep.

Since several of our flying customers lived off the highway, they

163

couldn't take their cars home with them. Over the years, we accumulated quite a parking lot full of vehicles. The Milanowskis, who came to Tetlin from Michigan with the Wycliffe Bible Translators shortly after we left the village, made frequent trips into Fairbanks. They would arrange to fly out with Marvin on a mail day, stay overnight with us, and drive on into town the next morning.

Bob and Molly McCombe, who had South Fork Lodge up on the Taylor Highway for many years, likewise left their car at our place through the winter months when the highway was closed. During the years Bob was in the Legislature he would drive the car down the Taylor just before the road closed and leave it with us. Then in January when the Legislature convened, Marvin would fly them out from South Fork, and when they came back in the spring, their car was ready for them. Larry Folger, a big game guide up at Chisana, left his vehicle parked at Cathedral, too. So when he wanted to make mid-winter trips to Anchorage for supplies, Marvin would pick him up in Chisana; and by the time they reached Cathedral, our boys would have his car all warmed up for him.

Father Bakewell, headquartered at the Catholic church in Delta, made weekly trips to several other parishes, including Tok, Northway, and Eagle. He loved airplanes and bear hunting, and had occasion to do a lot of flying. We got well-acquainted with him.

The Christmas of 1967 he made what seemed at first an impossible request. He wanted Marvin to pick him up in Delta Christmas morning right after his seven o'clock Mass. From there they would make stops and hold Christmas services at every one of his parishes, while Marvin stood by for him. This was going to be an all-day project, starting before dawn, and finishing long after dark. It meant that Marvin would be away from home all Christmas day. But he wasn't in the habit of turning down a flight, especially where it concerned Father Bakewell. So we had to find a solution.

Marvin had it. "We'll get up at four o'clock Christmas morning and open our gifts before I leave at seven. How's that?"

"Oh good," Cyndie beamed. "I've always wanted to get up at

four in the morning and open gifts!''

We not only had our gifts all opened in plenty of time, but then Marvin decided he wanted a sit-down breakfast with his whole family before he left. So at six o'clock we had bacon with an omelette, and we all went outdoors to watch the plane take off for Delta. By the time it got back late that afternoon, Christmas dinner was on the table, and we hadn't missed a beat. Father hadn't missed a single stop either, and a lot of people were happier that day for his having been there.

Niki Threlkheld, a petite little lady with a most unusual artistic ability, spent her entire married life following her husband from country to country as he worked for the World Bank. Her art work had been just a hobby. But after his untimely death when she was still a young woman, she turned her hobby into a means of making a living. She was a devout Catholic, and Father Bakewell encouraged her to come to Alaska to paint.

Her special talent was water color, and her special subjects were wild flowers. Niki painted flowers from one end of Alaska to the other over a period of several years. Marvin flew her up into the high country and mountain tops where she collected species of flowers never seen at the lower levels. With tent and camping gear, she sometimes sat on a little folding stool painting flowers in their natural habitat. If conditions were too rough to warrant that, she carefully wrapped her plants in damp cloth or paper and brought them back home to be painted.

One fall, on her way back to the east coast with her precious portfolio of paintings in a suitcase, her baggage was stolen and she lost her whole summer's work. The next spring she came back to Alaska and spent the entire summer duplicating every picture.

From 1964 until 1968, John and Cynthia Bridgers operated a store in Eagle. The road was open from spring until fall, but during the winter months Marvin air-freighted all their supplies in for them. John brought some of his supplies, including dry goods, all the way up from Missouri in a pickup truck. He'd help Marvin load the plane from our end of the line; and Cynthia, running a snow machine back and forth between the airstrip and their store, took care of the freight at the Eagle end. Thousands of pounds of food and clothing made its way to Eagle during those years.

CHAPTER XVIII

The float plane wasn't making its way. Not only was it cumbersome, but the Tanana was a poor place to keep it tied down. Flying season was short, too. We couldn't get it into the water until about the first of June because of ice on the lakes, and we had to pull it out early enough in September so it wouldn't get too cold to start the motor. Marvin began to think seriously of selling it and getting his chopper license.

But we had a chopper pilot up here in June, and after that I didn't hear much more about adding a helicopter to the fleet.

The Bureau of Land Management was surveying nearly two million acres of land between Tok and Delta that year and had a camp set up down at Tanacross. They hired two choppers from Rick Helicopters in California. One of the pilots made it up here all right; but the other one crashed two choppers before he finally got through to Alaska. He made his first forced landing down in Washington, but set down on a mountainside and rolled over sideways. So he went back to California to pick up a second one and had another motor failure at Williams Lake up in B.C. There he rolled down another mountainside, and by this time had done a total of thirteen thousand dollars in damage. But Rick had to have a chopper in Tanacross, so they sent him back with a third one, and that time he made it. They had told him they were sending him to Fairbanks, and he didn't realize the camp was in Tanacross. He was low on gas when he flew over Cathedral, so when he saw the airstrip and some planes there, he set down to refuel.

The pilot was definitely shook up, so came in for a cup of coffee.

"Where are you taking this thing anyway?" Marvin asked him.

"To Fairbanks, if my luck holds out long enough to get it there! What have I got left--about three hours of flying? The Bureau of Land Management has it chartered for the summer."

"Are you sure you should be going to Fairbanks? You know there's a BLM camp right down here at Tanacross, and they already have a chopper there. They're doing a big survey job between here and Delta this summer."

The man shook his head. "Do you suppose they don't even know where they're sending me? With the luck I've had on this trip, I wouldn't be surprised at anything."

So he phoned his headquarters in Anchorage, and was sent back to Tanacross.

They put him right to work the next day. The choppers were taking two surveyors at a time up into the Alaska Range where they dropped them off to stake and survey a two-mile-square plot of land, and then be picked up again and moved on to a new spot.

That first night on the job, this pilot with his two surveyors was just coming in for a landing at Tanacross. A bottle of mosquito dope packed in a wooden box on the skid blew up and shattered the box, and everything inside caught on fire. The three fellows didn't know what had happened, but they had flames shooting up the side of the chopper past the window. They got down as fast as they could, and all three of them piled out into a heap on the ground.

The next day their supervisor telephoned every BLM camp in Alaska and told them to get rid of their pressurized bottles of mosquito dope. And that night Marvin opened up his survival gear and confiscated the bottle of mosquito dope he had been carrying in the plane all summer.

Tetlin still had mail service just one day a week, on Tuesday. The chances were six to one that some of their Christmas mail would be piled up in the Tok post office until after the holiday. So Marvin had established a habit of making a free run into the village every year either the day before Christmas or on Christmas morning to be sure none of the presents got there late.

But Christmas came on Tuesday that year. The postmistress didn't want to be bothered with mail on Christmas day, so asked Marvin if he would fly it in on Monday instead. That was fine with us, because it precluded making that free trip. Marvin checked with the postmistress at Tetlin a week ahead of time to be sure she was agreeable to the idea, and of course she was. But then she was called away from the village, and had to turn her duties over to someone else.

Monday morning we woke up to sleet, and weather not fit for a plane to fly. But 36 Tango flew anyway, and the load of mail went to Tetlin. No one seemed to know who was supposed to be in charge. They got nasty about the plane's coming on a non-scheduled day and refused to open the post office and release the outgoing mail.

"That's fine with me," Marvin agreed. "I'll take this planeload of mail I have here back to Tok and bring it in tomorrow again if weather permits. But," he warned, "if I can't get in tomorrow and the village has to go without its Christmas mail, don't blame me!" Finally the post office was opened.

Because of the time spent squabbling, the plane was all covered with sleet. Marvin managed to get out of Tetlin, but landed in Tok and spent the rest of the day sitting out the weather at the Roberts' house. They finally heated up pans of water, and cleaned the wings off before Marvin could get in the air again.

Marvin had done more flying in 1962 than in any one year's time before. There were lots of trips in and out of Tetlin - not just on mail runs, but the passenger load was increasing. Mining and prospecting either were picking up or men were just resigning themselves to more flying and less tramping. Women were no longer having their babies delivered in the villages. We were flying them into Fairbanks or Glenallen to the hospital, and then flying them back again. Other medical cases were more commonly being flown, too. Government personnel were constantly on the move. Both the Bureau of Indian Affairs and the Bureau of Land Management were heavily staffed and active in village affairs and fire patrol.

The state Fish and Game Commission with a game warden stationed at Tok, added a biologist. There was a real increase in the hours of flying Marvin did on caribou counts in the Fortymile country. Caribou crossed the Taylor Highway by the thousands every fall, and the biologists started a massive project of air surveillance to establish a pattern in their migrations, their grazing areas, and their natural predators.

We couldn't keep up with the hundred hour inspections on the planes, and buying used aircraft was no longer practical. They were wearing out too fast. Every time we had to make a trade, it involved dozens of phone calls all over the lower states, delays, and costly trips. We were ready to justify that brand new airplane we had long talked about.

Marvin wanted to deal again with Mr. Mifflin in Spokane. He had been more than fair with us on 36 Tango; and his pilot, Frank Girault, who had ferried Tango up the highway route for us, wanted to come again. Tango was ready now for a major overhaul, and Mifflin gave us a price of two thousand dollars to do the job. Marvin thought that was a little stiff and we could probably get it done piecemeal locally a little cheaper. Besides, Marvin didn't know when he would have time to go out and pick it up once it was finished.

But we had to get Frank back to Spokane some way or other, so when Mifflin agreed to let Frank bring Tango back for us after the overhaul, we decided to send it south.

Since there was going to be transportation both ways, we invited Frank's wife to come up with him. By the time all these arrangements were made, it was the first part of March before the Giraults finally arrived with 20 Zulu-a shiny white and red, brand new Cessna 180. We spent a fun-filled two days showing them around the country, and when they finally took off for Seattle with Tango, Marvin felt a pit in his stomach. No one but he had ever flown the plane since we bought it, so this was the first time he had ever seen it in the air.

By the end of March, Frank had Tango back in Alaska for us, and we became basically a 180 air service. Delta still stayed on floats during the summer months, but became only a back-up otherwise. And Marvin had logged 3800 hours.

That summer of 1963, Helen Foster and her crew of geologists were doing work for the military, so they had military support. Two big banana choppers with a crew of four men for each machine moved into Cathedral Bluffs. Our two little Cessnas tied along the edge of the airstrip were dwarfed by the size of those immense machines. They took up most of the field, so that summer our flying had to be off the highway.

Just the year before that, Wiens had crash-landed a Cessna 180 up in the Seventymile country. They had taken out the engine and instruments, but left the plane there. Marvin gave them fifty dollars for it just as it sat.

Everyone had ideas as to how we could get it out of there. A family of miners who spent the summer in that part of the country said they would bring it out on skids behind their cat when they walked it out in the fall. But they didn't do it. One of the RCA boys at Delta had his eye on a snow-go he wanted to buy. He figured he and Marvin could go in overland with that and haul the plane out. But that didn't come to pass either. Marvin even considered going in from Eagle by dog team and bringing it out on those sleds he made to bring 79 Delta out from the hourglass lake. Remembering our experiences with dog teams during that disastrous affair though, discouraged us in a hurry.

Those two bananas on the strip at Cathedral turned out to be the answer. The crews, sitting around the counter every evening over cups of coffee soon learned the story about the plane up in the Seventymile. They wanted some excitement, so decided they could lift it out.

"We could take the wings off and strap them together," someone remarked.

"Or better yet," came another suggestion, "strap them right to the sides of the fuselage and sling the whole thing out in one trip."

"Do you think the Air Force would let you do it?" Marvin queried.

"They're always looking for practice exercises. Where could you find a better one?"

They finally decided that Marvin should request permission to have the job done.

171

"Who would I contact?" Marvin asked. "Your Major in Anchorage?"

"No!" one of the pilots explained. "You never start from the bottom and go up. You start from the top and come down."

Bob Bartlett, they decided, was the man to go to. Bob had been our delegate to Congress during our Territorial years; and once we became a state, he was elected to the Senate. He was an old-timer in Alaska, knew half his constituents by name, and had visited us on several occasions both at Unalakleet and Cathedral Bluffs.

Marvin wrote Bob a detailed letter explaining what we wanted. Bob got right with it, and in short order the request not only sifted down to the Major in Anchorage, but they gave us the green light. They would charge us just the expense incurred, we were told, and came forth with a figure of $204.16.

Supposedly only one of the choppers was to go. But by the time everything got put together, they decided they would have to take two. Marvin had signed an agreement that if the load began to swing too much in mid-air, they were authorized to cut it loose. But how would they know how much it was swinging if they couldn't watch it from another aircraft? So in the end, both choppers went to the Seventymile. They strapped the wings to the side of the fuselage of the 180, wrapped it in a sling, and with Marvin riding in the second chopper beside them, they carried it into Eagle. From there we trucked it down the Taylor Highway to Cathedral Bluffs where it still sits in the boneyard. It supplied a few spare parts now and then, but with all our good intentions, it never got rebuilt.

Late that fall I was frying a hamburger for a customer at the counter when the phone rang. Spatula in hand, I ran to the phone just on the other side of the kitchen door.

"Mrs. Warbelow?" a man's voice at the other end queried.

"Yes."

"This is Bob Bartlett."

"Bob Bartlett! Where are you?"

"Oh, I'm here in Washington. I just got to wondering - did

172

Marv ever get that plane out of the Seventymile?"

I was thoroughly embarrassed to think that we hadn't even been considerate enough to let him know the outcome of the plane story. So while my hamburger burned black, I assured him we had the plane and were grateful for his help. That night Marvin sat down and wrote the letter he should have written months before.

Cathedral Bluffs was a natural as a take-off point for hunters. Dall sheep roamed the mountainsides of the Johnson, Robertson, Little Tok, and Gerstle Rivers. Moose and caribou were fair game, and grizzlies hung out in the high country, too. Marvin, by 1963, had already built up a sizeable clientele of hunters, using the 170 on floats and a 180 on wheels. But neither of these planes was suitable for sandbar landing in sheep country. The time had come to add a Super Cub to the fleet.

Marvin had agreed to take four grizzly hunters out about the first of June, so that forced the issue. We located a plane, just a year old, and in good condition, down in Denver.

"Can you have it up here before June first?" Marvin asked. "I've got four bear hunters to take out and no plane to take them with."

"Send me a down payment, and it will be on its way," he was told.

We sent the money, but no plane appeared. Marvin finally phoned again. "Where's my Cub?" he wanted to know.

"We've decided to put a new windshield in it before we send it. The old one is pretty badly scratched."

This concerned us a little bit. We thought we were buying a fairly new plane in good shape. Why would it have a windshield that had to be replaced, we wondered.

In the meantime June 1 came, and so did the four hunters. Marvin and the boys did a hurry-up job of pulling the 170 out of the water and skidding it up the river road to a tripod they had rigged up the summer before. They got the floats off and wheels on in record time, and put the plane to work. Our hunters had come and gone before the Cub ever arrived.

A few days later our little red and white PA 18 went through

Customs at Northway and we got a phone call to meet the pilot in Tanacross. Very few pilots ever landed on our short strip at Cathedral, with the hump in the middle and obstacles at both ends, if there was anywhere else to go. Marvin picked up his new plane in Tanacross to fly it home, and 32 Zulu became an essential part of our operation.

That little Cub had a rocky beginning. On June 18, Marvin gave Ron an hour's instruction, but then didn't get it off the ground again for several days. The night of July 10, a big fire broke out up at Crooked Creek. Marvin spent all night and most of the next day ferrying men and equipment out of Eagle to the fire. He didn't get home until mid-afternoon. He crawled right into bed, and was still sound asleep when LaMar Henry called him from Tok at midnight.

"Lavell went out this afternoon with that J3 of his, and didn't get back," LaMar explained. "I just went out with my 150 and located him. He's sitting up on a sandbar on the Little Tok with a busted prop."

Marvin was still groggy. "You say he's on the Little Tok? On a sandbar? Well, what do you want me to do?"

"Go up and get him! I'm afraid to land there."

"But I'll probably be afraid to land there too. I haven't done much flying in this Cub, you know. Anyway, it's pretty darned dark to be landing on a strange sandbar right now. If you think he'll be all right until daylight, I'll go up then."

LaMar flew back up the river to drop a sleeping bag and gun to Lavell and left him there for the night. The next morning at four o'clock, Marvin brought Lavell and his bent prop back to Tok.

Two days later they flew back and put a new prop on the J3. Since they weren't sure the plane hadn't had some damage done, Marvin flew cover all the way to Tok, where Lavell landed and Marvin started back to Cathedral. But at Tanacross he began to have motor trouble. He couldn't even get as far as the airfield. The motor gave out and he had to land on the access road leading off the Alaska Highway. We towed the Cub into the field with our pickup, and there it sat for three weeks while we had a new motor flown up from Oklahoma. Marvin and Bud Sutherland installed it, and 32 Zulu was back in action again.

CHAPTER XIX

Those years from 1963 on, were living nightmares interspersed with moments of sheer elation for two solid months during hunting season. Sheep season opened August 10, but our hunters always started moving in on us by the eighth; and there was no let-up for us until the last moose and caribou were brought in toward the end of September.

There were no guide requirements for hunting in our area, so we had more out-of-state hunters as a rule than we did residents. Marvin was always booked solid; so all it would take was one or two days of rain, fog, or wind, and we were fouled up for the rest of the season. Most hunters were on a limited vacation, so they'd arrive, wound up like eight day clocks, anticipating a trip into the hills within hours. Sometimes it worked out that way, and sometimes it didn't. If weather closed in on the mountains, they could be good sports about it for an hour or so. But by the time a half day went by, we'd have a cafe full of guys pacing the floor, looking out the windows at the range across the road, and checking their watches. If a second day rolled around and weather got no better, they would start looking for a target. Marvin was usually it.

That fall of 1964 started out on an upbeat. The first three days, we were able to get ten hunters into the hills. Then came two days of high winds. Marvin couldn't even get to Gold King with the 180, say nothing about a sandbar on the Robertson River with the Cub. I made pots of coffee and Marvin spun his usual round of hunting stories from previous years, but there was a limit to how long you could appease a bunch of fellows whose time was running out when they hadn't even yet started.

Finally on the third day, the storm subsided. Marvin got up at two-thirty that morning and began moving men out. He got his last three into their spots and brought out the first of his hunters ready to come in. They had their sheep, fortunately. I think if they had come in empty-handed, Marvin would have been ready to ditch the whole thing.

By seven o'clock, he was out of the Cub and ready to take off in the 180 for Gold King. Our three boys were an essential part of the operation. Not only could they push one plane into its parking spot and tie it down, but they always had the second plane gassed and ready to go.

The whole place was hunter-oriented every fall. We cleared everyone out of the bunkhouse and turned it over to the hunters those two months. If they got in a day ahead of time, they could roll a bag out on a bunk for the night. It was a handy place to spread out their gear and rearrange their packs. We had a hard and fast rule that the packs couldn't exceed fifty pounds. One man and his limited gear was all the Cub could handle on those short, rough bars along rivers.

The fellows could use the bunkhouse again when they got in from their hunts. If they wanted to stay over an extra night or even a whole extra day to salt down their meat and get it bagged, they had a place to do it.

Two men came up the highway from the mid-west one fall for a flight out the next day. They unpacked in the bunkhouse, then came up to the cafe to get acquainted and eat a meal. On the way, they had stopped to take a look at the Cub.

"I don't think you'll ever get all our gear in that little plane in one load," one of them commented.

By mid-season, Marvin was usually carrying quite a chip on his shoulder. "I'd better be able to get it in one load! What makes you think I can't?"

"We've got an awful lot of stuff."

Marvin walked down to the bunkhouse to take a look at their

piles of gear. He came blustering back.

"Good gosh, man! What do you think you're going to do with all that junk? You've got a slab of bacon, loaves of bread, fresh eggs in cartons! I thought you said you knew something about hunting and backpacking!"

"Oh, we aren't going to backpack all that stuff. We'll set up base camp and just leave it there while we hunt."

"Well, you're right when you said it couldn't go in on one trip. So you'd better start paring right now! I told you I'd limit you to fifty pounds each."

The two fellows were dismayed. "But you said in your letter that any excess baggage would be fifty cents a pound."

"Of course I said it. That's prohibitive. Any guy should be able to figure out that meant they didn't bring any excess."

"But we're willing to pay fifty cents a pound! You'll just have to make an extra trip."

"I'm not making any extra trips if you paid me ten dollars a pound! I'm on a tight schedule and I've got a mob of fellows who will be here tomorrow morning to fly out. It isn't the money. It's the time. I think we'd better all go down to the bunkhouse with the scales and start sorting."

In a huff, all three of them stormed out the door. But by the time they got to the bunkhouse, the situation had already been resolved. They met Pepper, our Shetland pony, just coming out the end of the building with the last half of a loaf of bread in his mouth and raw egg smeared all over his whiskers. The slab of bacon, chewed to pieces, lay on the floor behind him. Gear and food were strung all over their bunkroom. By the time they had salvaged what they could, there was no more problem about weight limit.

We had sold our last Cessna 170 to the teacher up a Eagle, and during the summer of 1965, the Cub had replaced it as a float plane.

Hunting season slipped up on us sooner than we expected. Every year, Marvin insisted he wouldn't book so full, but it didn't do any good. Booked or not, when August came, we had hunters all over the place.

All of a sudden we realized we were in a world of trouble. We needed the Cub on floats for part of our operation, and on wheels for the other part.

Some fellow in Anchorage had a 1961 Cub with two radios and big tires, looking for a buyer. Marvin called and told him that if he could have it up here the next day, we'd take it. That was the quickest deal we ever made. The pilot missed by just one day. We made our first call Monday, and by Wednesday noon we had a little orange PA 18 - 84 Zulu - sitting on our strip. That afternoon it began to fly hunters.

Cliff Jenkins from Fairbanks had been coming out every season for his sheep hunt, but usually walked instead of flying in. Cathedral was about the closest spot for the walkers to start from, so some of the hunters in the hills didn't fly with us; but we kept track of them and occasionally made supply drops.

This year Cliff brought his twelve-year-old son with him on his first sheep hunt. Cliff didn't want the boy to carry a pack, so they left most of their gear with us. With an early morning start, they planned to be at their base camp by noon, and Marvin was to make a drop there for them. That was the day before our new Cub arrived, and Marvin was hamstrung as far as flying hunters was concerned, so he had plenty of time to do Cliff's drop for him. But high winds kept him out of the hills all day. About six-thirty that evening it calmed down, so he took the door off a 180; and with Ron in the back seat to push baggage out, they got up to Cliff's campsite. Cliff wasn't to be seen; but they assumed he had gone out exploring, so they made the drop anyway. By the time they got back to home base, Cliff and his boy were already here. They had given up on Marvin and walked back to Cathedral. There was no way we could salvage their duffels for them, so the next morning they walked back in again.

Marvin took a couple of fellows one fall on to a nasty little strip out back of Delta. He hadn't ever landed there, and wasn't sure he could. So just to be on the safe side, he took only gear in on that first trip, dumped it, and went back for his men. By the time he got back with his first passenger, a grizzly and her cub had taken up squatter's rights beside the gear. They had to circle for twenty minutes trying to scare her off, while she reared into the air and clawed and bellowed at them. But she finally got tired of the game and moved on. Marvin landed, but wouldn't get out of the plane until the man behind him had crawled out and had his gun in hand.

Grizzlies were a common problem, expecially to sheep hunters. The men usually had to do a lot of climbing into high country from their camps in order to bag a sheep. Then the trip back down was always a rugged one, so they'd have to stash the meat while they climbed down to camp with the head and horns. More than once a hunter would get back to his kills, only to find that a grizzly had beat him to it. Sometimes the fellows could store the meat in a tree until they got back, but too often there wasn't a tree available.

Most men who go out are there for the outing as well as the hunt. If they get some decent weather and a lot of hiking, but don't bag any game, they will be good sports about it. We seldom had a disgruntled hunter. But once in a while it happened.

There was this fellow and his partner from Fairbanks. Since most of our hunters were from Outside, Marvin picked his spots to drop them in. He had just so many places where he could land, so as soon as he brought one party out of a hunting spot, he took another one in. The plans were all made before season ever opened, and any juggling later made for problems.

Marvin had these two men booked for a spot on the Gerstle River. Nothing had been said up to this point about where they were going. Suddenly one man realized where he was.

"This doesn't show me anything!" he shouted into Marvin's ear from the rear seat. "I've hunted up here before!"

Marvin didn't know quite what he was driving at. "Oh, you have? Well then you know there's a lot of sheep up here."

The man was irked. "I don't intend to pay good money to hunt a place I already know. I figured I'd see some new country."

"Then why didn't you tell me when you set this hunt up that you wanted to pick your own spot?" Marvin shouted back. "It's too late to change plans now. Anyway, I didn't guarantee to show you country you'd never seen before. I guaranteed to show you sheep. And I've got your partner in there already. He didn't do any complaining about where he was going.''

"Of course he didn't. He's never been here before.''

Marvin set down on a stretch of gravel on the north side of the river where his first passenger was waiting for them. The second one was furious, but no way would Marvin move them to a new spot.

"And whatever you do,'' were his parting words as he crawled back into the plane, "don't cross that river! It's fairly low right now, but the water can come up any minute and there's no place on the other side where I can pick you up. You could get trapped over there.''

Two days later when he flew over to check on them, there stood the two fellows on the south bank waving him down. Marvin of course, was aggravated and considered just flying off and leaving them. But then he had second thoughts about it, so he circled again and sat down across the river from them at their campsite. He crawled out of the plane, cupped his hands around his mouth and yelled across at them, "What the devil are you doing over there anyway?''

"What do you think we're doing?'' one of them called back. We're looking for sheep! Why the deuce didn't you land over here so you could pick us up? You can't do us any good over there!''

"I told you I couldn't land over there! You'd better get yourselves back on this side.''

"We got soaking wet coming over and the river is higher now than it was this morning. If you're too chicken to get us out of here, maybe you can at least bring our bags and some grub over for us.''

"I won't land there even for that. But if you want me to drop some stuff to you, I will.

They settled for that, and gave Marvin instructions as to which pieces of duffel to drop and which to leave. Marvin made the drop, but as luck would have it, they forgot they had a dozen fresh eggs in one of the bags. They had raw egg splattered all over.

By the time Marvin went back a few days later to haul them out, they had managed to get themselves back to the north side of the river, but they were no longer on speaking terms with him. Even the fact that they had two big sets of horns didn't sweeten things up.

The Major and First Lieutenant didn't fare so well either. They too, came out from Fairbanks. The Lieutenant had made all the arrangements ahead of time, and was extremely uptight by the time they reached Cathedral. He wanted to be sure nothing would go wrong that might displease the Major.

He motioned Marvin outdoors to talk to him. "This hunt means an awful lot to the Major. But you know he's not a young man, and I'm afraid this backpacking in the hills might be a little rough for him."

"Of course it's going to be rough. I told you that in the beginning," Marvin pointed out. "If you think he can't make it, then you'd better not let him go in the first place."

"Well, I was wondering if you might be able to take us up there without our sleeping bags and then drop them to us after we've picked out a camping spot?"

Marvin didn't think much of the idea. "I have a policy of never taking a man out without his gear. What if I drop you off and then kill myself before I have a chance to get back with your bags?"

The Lieutenant was surprised. "You don't intend to do that, do you?"

In the end, the Lieutenant got his way. They went back into the cafe to tell the Major their plans. That was fine with him.

"But I like to take one fellow out for a look around to get the lay of the land first," Marvin said. "Which one of you wants to go?"

"Take the Major. He'll enjoy the trip," the younger man replied.

The Major was enjoying the trip immensely until all of a sudden a dozen white sheep came into view along the hillside. He leaned out the window for a better view and whoosh-away went his bifocals! Marvin was aghast.

"Oh, that's all right," the Major assured him good naturedly. "I can get a new pair for four dollars."

Marvin set his two men down on a bar along the river, and arranged to come back in four hours with the two bags tied together, ready to drop.

He spotted the hunters a good way up the mountain, let down into a tight circle, and dropped the bags right above them. But the bundle got hung up on the strut, and although it stuck there only a matter of seconds before it broke loose, it didn't land where it was supposed to. Marvin had no way of communicating with them, so all he could do was to spot the bags from the air, and circle until the men located them. He circled until he was sure they were on the right track. The gear had landed in a cleared area and he thought would be quite visible.

They never found the bags. Marvin went back the next day to check on them and found them huddled on the river bar, cold as icebergs. They had had a miserable night and hadn't even got near a sheep. Relations were strained when they packed up and left for home, and there wasn't much we could do to make them better. The thing had happened, and that was just the way it was.

"I learned one lesson from all this," Marvin concluded. "That's the last time I take a man out without his sleeping bag in hand."

CHAPTER XX

Early in the spring of 1964 we had some correspondence with the president of the Harvard University Mountain Climbing Club. Some of the fellows had climbed Mt. McKinley the previous year and were planning another summer on both Mt. Hayes and Mt. Deborah out in the Gold King area. They made arrangements for Marvin to drop their supplies for them at various levels along the route. One of the questions they had asked was the maximum size box we could get into the 180 and Marvin gave them that dimension.

Two of them - the president and his companion, left Harvard minutes after their last final and drove non-stop across country and up the Alaska Highway with a pickup load of gear. They were overly tired and still uptight from final tests when they reached Cathedral Bluffs. The boys were both small, trim and in good shape. They were ready to start out that same day.

"You don't look to me as though you're ready to start our right now," Marvin insisted. "I think you need a night's rest and some time to unwind before we get going on this project."

"We're ready right now," they insisted. "If we're going to get to the tops of two mountains, we don't have any time to waste. Your summers up here are too short. Besides, we have some more fellows coming up later to make the Hayes climb with us, so we have a date to meet. If we can just get these drops made today, we should be ready to start climbing tomorrow morning."

"Okay," Marvin shrugged. "It's your necks. So let's take a look at your gear and figure out what I'm supposed to drop and where."

They all walked out to the little pickup with the Massachusetts license plate all covered with mud, and it was then Marvin discovered that they had the whole back of it full of great big boxes. Every one was maximum size.

Marvin was floored. "Good gosh, boys, what do you think I'm going to do with all these great big boxes?"

One was a cocky little fellow, and he bristled right now. "Big boxes? I asked you how big a box you could get in that plane, and you told me. So here they are. There isn't one here that exceeds your measurements."

"I know. I know. You asked me what the maximum size was that I could handle, but I had no idea you intended to pack them all that big! If you climbed McKinley last year, then you should have some idea of how an airplane is shaped, and how a pilot loads one. Sure, I could get one of those boxes in, but that's all. Everything else that I pack around it is going to have to be a lot smaller."

The boys, arms folded, hung over the edge of the pickup in silence, irritated, and waiting for Marvin to change his mind. He didn't. Each one tried to out-silence the other.

Finally Marvin turned to go back to the cafe. "I've got lots of boxes here; if you want me to do your flying, you'll have to start repacking."

They didn't like it, but they had no other choice. They spent the rest of the day rearranging their gear into smaller boxes.

We had a crew of BLM sky divers there that summer, some of them surveying state land, and other diving out of the chopper to clear out heliports for future landings. They crowded around the mountain climbers and watched in amazement at the stuff they saw being shuttled from big boxes to little ones. Most impressive were the coils of thin nylon rope and the sharp little spikes they would use as steps along the sheer walls.

The jumpers were still in a state of shock when they came in for dinner that evening. The two climbers were their main topic of conversation.

186

"Did you see that rope?" one of them asked aghast. "Boy-oh-boy, give me a chute any day!"

The mountain climbers were all ready to go that night, but by the next morning they decided they didn't have the right kind of radio equipment, so they made a trip into Fairbanks to get what they needed. By the time they got back the following day, the Alaska Range was buried in clouds. The boys began to pace like caged lions, and I think they figured it was Marvin's fault. They almost had me thinking it, too.

"Don't worry about them," Marvin whispered on a trip through the kitchen. "They needed a cooling-off period anyway."

The fourth morning after their arrival, the stage was set. Weather cleared, the radio was working, and boxes were all packed. They decided one would go with Marvin on his two flights to drop their supplies.

They made a successful first drop, but the second one further up wasn't so good. They had packed some matches in one of the boxes, and when it hit the ground, a match must have struck just right, because it caught fire and the whole box burned up. Because it took some time for the fire to get going, Marvin and Don didn't realize what had happened. The boys didn't find it out until they reached that campsite on their way up the mountain.

On their third and last drop, Marvin circled, and then shouted to the boy in the back sea, "Push!"

The whole cabin suddenly filled with loose down floating all around. Marvin's heart missed a beat. "I've lost him!" he thought. "The kid went out the door with the box!" And almost at the same instant, it occurred to him that there was nothing he could do about it.

He turned around cautiously, almost afraid to look. There sat the boy with one hand clapped over the other arm.

"I wrecked my jacket!" he moaned. "Caught the sleeve on something sharp!"

We thought the boys ought to wait until the next morning to start their climb, but there was no stopping them now that the supplies were landed. With a patch on the one boy's sleeve, they climbed into the plane and Marvin flew them to the base of Mt. Deborah where they started their climb.

CHAPTER XXI

1969 wasn't a good year. The world seemed at odds with itself. We started out the summer with droughts and high winds. By July the whole state was burning up. Forest fires were out of control in every direction.

Marvin flew fire patrol for seventeen days almost nonstop. The Bureau of Land Management had him on a twelve-hour-a-day schedule. He'd fly four hours at a stretch, with two hours in between flights to catch a nap. This worked out all right except that he still had other flying that wouldn't wait. Most of that he had to do between midnight and eight in the morning.

Ron was working for the Geological Survey that summer and doing a lot of chopper flying with Helen Foster. Smoke was so thick in the Fortymile country that, instead of doing their rock collecting where they wanted to, they did it wherever the smoke would allow them to go. Even Marvin and the BLM planes couldn't get places where they should have. They, too, had to skirt the smoke. Every available vehicle in the country had been leased to the BLM-trucks, pickups, jeeps, cats, - everything.

That hot, dry summer ended abruptly, and winter came the same way. There was no autumn in between. We hardly had the smoke of the forest fires cleared out of our lungs in time for the first blizzard. It hit us on August 7 and went on without a let-up for five days. Snow, high winds, and freezing temperatures such as we had never seen that time of year. Sheep hunters started congregating the morning of the eighth. By the tenth, we were mobbed. But it wasn't until late that afternoon that Marvin was able to start flying them out. We had two parties waiting here that had women in them. He finally talked them into cancelling out completely because he didn't think the girls could cope with the snow and cold they would find up in the high country.

Helen Foster had been doing most of her flying during the summer with a chopper they had under contract. But choppers never took chances on staying around too late in the fall, so hers was gone by mid-July. She and her assistant, Jo Laird, were flying the Cub again. Jo had proved to be a match for the Fortymile, so those two went on long backpack trips. Marvin took them out about the twentieth of July, and on the twenty-sixth he moved them to the Middle Fork on the Fortymile River. Five days later he picked them up again and dropped them off at North Fork. He made their next move on August 5. Each time he met them, he took in fresh supplies they had packaged and labelled ahead of time, and backhauled the rocks they had collected. Their next trek was to be the longest one yet. They planned to hike and hunt rocks for seven days, and have the plane bring in more supplies on August 12, up at the Kink, about twenty miles as the crow flies, north of Chicken.

During the short lull between the end of fire season and the beginning of hunting season, two old Jewish fellows from New York stopped in looking for a fly-in fishing trip. It was a little late for good fishing. But they were all equipped with a tent, and camping and fishing gear, and we still had one of the Cubs on floats, so Marvin took them in to T Lake for a three-day outing.

Then came the storm on August seventh. Not only did we have a pile-up of hunters, but we were concerned about Helen and Jo.

"They're a tough pair of ladies," we agreed, "but they aren't prepared for a snowstorm."

"There isn't anything I can do about it now," Marvin had to admit. "I have no idea where they are. The best I can do is be darned sure I'm at the Kink on the twelfth. They've never missed a time and place yet, and I don't think they will this time. I'm the one who will have a problem getting there."

By the night of the eleventh, our immediate pile-up of hunters were out in their camps. The morning of the twelfth we were back to another snowstorm, but Marvin made the Tetlin mail run on schedule.

The boys had 32 Zulu ready when he got home. Helen's last pack of supplies was loaded, and the gas tanks were full. The boys had heated the motor, and as soon as they heard the hum of the 180 off in the direction of Tok, they got the tiedowns off the Cub.

Marvin had a rough trip in a miserable snowstorm ahead of him. He planned to meet the girls with their supplies and some warm clothes I had sent along for them, then come home as quickly as possible.

The girls were waiting for Marvin, as he knew they would be. The river at the Kink didn't have a suitable spot along the shore where he could put the plane down, so he had to settle for a sandbar in the middle of the river.

Helen and Jo were cold and wet. With all the snow, there was no possible way they could do any more geology work. There was nothing for Marvin to do but get them out of there. They waded to the sand bar, both climbed into the back seat, and packed their backpacks around them.

There had been no let-up in the snowfall. If anything, it was getting heavier. The sandbar was short, the plane overloaded, and visibility was so poor Marvin couldn't see the end of the bar.

They sat there for an hour waiting for a let-up in the storm, and during this time Marvin and Helen, using Jo's rainpants as a blanket, cleaned the snow off the wings twice. With Helen on one side of the wing and Marvin the other, they pulled the pants the full length of it and rubbed the wing clean. The snow was wet and heavy, and inclined to ball up and stick to the wings as the pants slid over them.

Finally they noted a slight letup in the snowfall and decided the time had come to attempt a take-off. They pulled the rain pants along the wings once more, and got back into the plane as quickly as possible. But already the snow fall was thickening again.

As they rolled down the gravel bar, Marvin tried to bounce the plane off the ground, and he was so close on his last attempt that it looked as though they were going to make it. But at the end of the bar they still didn't have quite enough flying speed. They lifted into the air briefly, and then the wheels touched the water. Again they lifted, and a second time the plane settled and the wheels spit water. Marvin's only hope was that he could make it to the next little sandbar ahead of them, but a cliff just off the edge of the river was probably creating a downdraft for him. The plane touched water three or four times before they finally lost all possibility of getting enough flying speed to stay in the air, and they settled down in the middle of the river.

Stunned, they sat in silence for a few seconds. Helen was the first to speak.

"Well, I guess we've had it!"

Marvin was silent.

After a few more uncomfortable seconds, Helen said again, "Well, I guess we've had it!" and Marvin repeated, "Yes, I guess we've had it."

Then he added, "We're sitting right on the bottom of the river, so there's no need for us to hurry real fast."

But the plane was rapidly filling with water and their loose gear was floating out the window and down stream. After seeing a couple of duffels disappear, including the one that had in it Helen's new long all-wool Swiss underwear she had never worn, they began securing the rest of their load to keep from losing that, too.

Finally, they all climbed out into the river and hanging on to a wing, they followed it into shallow water and then waded to shore. Then, with Marvin in the deep water nearest the plane, Helen in the middle, and Jo close to shore, they formed a line and handed the gear from one to another to safety on the river bank.

They managed to get a fire going, and Jo who was suffering the most from the cold, started trying to dry out while Marvin and Helen waded back into the torrent of icy water in an attempt to save the plane. With the craft full of water, their pushing and tugging was useless. Every few minutes they had to go back to shore to warm up a bit and then give it another try. Marvin was reluctant to ask Jo for help, but they had no choice. She finally waded back into the river, and together all three of them, still taking brief periods to warm up, were able to push the plane to dry land. The prop was badly bent, a wing damaged, and the motor soaked. And of course, all of them were freezing and soaking wet.

Once they had the plane secured, they sorted out a minimum of gear, including meat bars for two day's rations, and stashed the remaining gear under the plane. It was nearing dark and still snowing hard. Helen's choice would have been to stay the night since they had a fire already built and a little shelter from surrounding trees. But Marvin wanted to get started for home, so they began walking.

Between them and Chicken, thirty miles or so away if you're on the ground, was a 5600 ft. mountain. Marvin had made his trip with as little clothing as possible because he knew he would be loaded with rocks the geologists had collected. With nothing but a flight jacket, low canvas shoes, and no cap or mittens, he was in no way equipped for the trip ahead of him. The girls were better dressed by far, and in better shape for hiking. Jo improvised a cap for Marvin from a plastic bag, and they did everything they could to ease the trip for him.

As they left the plane, they headed out along the banks of the Fortymile River. They walked as far as they could that night, and Helen finally convinced Marvin it would be better to stop and wait for some daylight.

"Then let's stop right here," Marvin suggested. "We're in a steep, dry gully where we'll get some protection from the wind."

But there was no place to get comfortable. They built a fire, and sat out the night. However, as the rain and snow continued, the gully became a stream. They had to keep moving to keep out of the water and to keep their fire from going out. No one got any sleep and very little rest.

The trio set out again at daylight, cutting across a broad, muskeg-covered terrace of the Fortymile River. They finally had to turn up a tributary and eventually head away from the river in order to locate the pass over into the Buckskin Creek drainage. While they were hopping from one huge boulder to another in the tributary, Marvin slipped down between two rocks and damaged his knee. This slowed him up for the rest of the trip.

With still no letup in the snow and rain, they now had to cope with a strong, cold wind that had come up. Helen finally decided they could no longer take the path of least resistance and had to climb over the top of the mountain. This was the roughest part of their trip because of deep snow, strong winds, and Marvin's crippled leg. The girls went on ahead following their map to the pass. Then while they waited for Marvin to catch up, they tried to check their map again to be sure they were heading down into the right drainage. Not only was it impossible to unfold the map, but they couldn't even stand up against the raging wind.

Once over the top, they dropped down into the valley on the other side, and just before dark they reached a miner's cabin closed up for the winter. They all had a lot of reservations about going in, but they had little choice. Inside this tiny structure were a bunk, one chair, a stove, and a can of beans.

Jo had suffered the most from that bout with the river, and couldn't seem to stop shivering. After the beans had been finished off, she curled up at the head of the bunk, Marvin at the foot, and Helen sat up all night in the chair with her feet propped up on the edge of the bunk, and kept the fire going. They slept, but not much.

The next day they walked an old cat trail on into Chicken. Their route took them by Art Purdy's cabin where they stopped in for a cup of cofee. Marvin could hardly wait to get that cup in his hands and really relished it. But Helen, who never touches coffee, had to drink a little just to be polite.

Cyndie and I and a dentist's family from Sacramento were alone at the lodge Tuesday night. The dentist, a friend of my brother in California, had planned to go on to Fairbanks that day. But when Marvin failed to show by late afternoon and we knew he had run into trouble, they decided to sit it out with us.

Classes at the University wouldn't start until the last part of August, so Ron was still working for the Geological Survey. Helen laid out work for him to do while she was gone, and that included making a trip up the Taylor Highway as far as Columbia Flats to take sediment samples. But since she didn't want him to go alone on account of bears all through that country, she had asked me to send the two younger boys with him. The boys had been gone for two or three days, and weren't due back until late

Wednesday.

We remembered the many times Marvin had told us, "Always give me twenty-four hours before you start looking for me." But when a plane is down, and you know it's down, you don't wait twenty-four hours.

At daybreak on Wednesday, Bob and Ellis Roberts in their Piper Family Cruiser and Bill Simmons with his Stinson were ready to go. But violent winds kept them on the ground most of the time. They finally, later in the day, were able to take off, and located the Cub tied down at the Kink. They looked for some sign on the ground that would indicate which way Marvin had gone, but there was none. Neither did they have any idea as to the whereabouts of the girls. They scouted the surrounding area with no luck, and then with the dark settling fast, and high winds still tossing them around, had to give up and come back to Tok.

Cyndie and I were pacing the floor, close to hysteria, long into the night, and the Elliott family was at a loss as to what to do about it. Finally, at midnight, the three boys pulled in at the front door. Cyndie was outside and jerked the car door open before Ron had turned off the motor.

"Dad, Dad!" she was crying. "Did you see Dad? Do you know where he is?"

Ron jumped out of the car and got her by the shoulders. "Cyndie! Stop this. Tell us what's happened!"

"Dad went to the Kink yesterday morning to meet the girls, and he didn't come back!" she sobbed.

All four of them piled into the cafe and we went into immediate conference.

"Bob and Ellis and Bill have looked for him all day," I told the boys. "They flew all the way to Chicken and can't find a sign of him. And we don't even know whether he ever found the girls or not!"

The boys were panicked. "I don't think they started toward Chicken at all," Ron insisted. "The shortest and most logical way out of the Kink would be to go toward Columbia Flats. We just came from there, and no way in the world could anyone walk through that snow up there. We've got to get a plane in the air at daylight and check out that route!''

I felt like a real crumb calling those three pilots out of bed at midnight, but I did it. I talked first to Bill.

"The boys just got home, Bill. Ron says he's sure Marvin is trying to walk out to Columbia Flats and there's too much snow up there for him to get through. Can you possibly get out again at daylight?''

Bill always kept his cool. "I'll get there as soon as I can, Lou. But I've got to have a little sleep, and then it will take me some time to gas up the plane. I don't have it ready to go.''

The kids were all crowded around me, their ears as close to the receiver as they could get.

"Tell him we'll take care of the plane for him," Ron whispered. "We'll have it ready as early as he wants it.''

They made the deal. The boys filled all our available jeep cans full of aviation gas, loaded them into the back of the pickup, and went to bed. By four o'clock, Cyndie and Ron were up again and on their way to Tok where Bill had his Stinson tied down on Roberts' airstrip just back of their house. When Bill got there a half hour later, the plane was gassed, cleared of ice and snow, and the ropes untied.

"I never had such service like this in my life!" Bill declared.

Ron wanted to fly with Bill and show him the route where he expected they would find his dad. But Bill turned him down.

"If I'm going up into that Fortymile, I want someone with me who knows every inch of the country. There isn't anyone who knows it better than Bob Roberts does. I'll take him with me.''

Bob was up, too, and ready to go. Ellis had decided not to go with them. Those two old fellows from New York sitting out on T Lake were by now two days overdue, and we had to get them out of there. That meant taking the Cub on floats, and Ellis was the most logical pilot to do it. He had a Piper on floats himself.

Bill and Bob were back within a couple of hours, and jubilant. They had spotted Marvin and the girls walking down the cat trail toward Chicken, probably another three or four hours from the

196

highway. I had packed some food for them to drop just in case they found someone, and with it a note asking Marvin if he wanted his boots dropped, too. But he signalled them a "no". His shoes had survived the mountain, and he didn't want the added weight of his boots.

The four young Warbelows were ready to explode with excitement. "We'll take Helen's car and go up the Taylor Highway to meet them!"

"No you won't!" Bill and Bob were emphatic. "We located them, and bigosh, we're going to bring them out in style!"

There was no point in arguing with them. They fired up two planes, and with great gusto were waiting at Chicken when the three trudged in off the end of the cat trail.

Mary met the planes when they taxied to a stop on the Roberts' airstrip, and greeted Marvin with a big hug.

"Marvin," she reminded him, "you should have left for the Bahamas a week ago like you said you would."

Once the two planes had taken off the landing strip and headed for Chicken, Ellis and the two kids brought the pickup back to Cathedral where Ellis fired up Marvin's float plane and made his first trip to T Lake.

He anticipated finding a couple of old men either frightened, or furious, or at least worried. But he wasn't prepared for what he really found. Their tent had caught on fire during one of those nights and burned to the ground. They had managed to save their sleeping bags and some food, so were camped out under the trees, and glad to see him. If they'd had any discomfort as a result of their predicament, they accepted it gracefully, and the audience they found waiting for them at Cathedral Bluffs far outweighed that discomfort.

We listened and watched in silent wonder while they dramatized the whole frightful story of leaving a fire in the stove when they went to bed, and waking up zipped inside their bags to find everything around them in flames. Wild-eyed, one of them told us how he fumbled with the zipper, finally wiggled free of his bag, and grabbed the pail of water he had brought in the night before. With his feet braced far apart, he reached for the imaginary pail, gave it a wild swing toward an imaginary camp stove, then stopped in mid-swing and looked at it in horror.

"I grab the pail of water - I give it a big throw - and then I look. Nothing! I have only ice!"

Once sheep hunting ended, a little of the pressure was off. We still had moose, caribou, and bear hunters roaming the country, but that was usually more low key. This gave us some time to think about the Cub sitting up at the Kink.

Marvin flew up there one day, hoping he might push the plane from the shore back to the sandbar where he had landed originally. But the water was over his boot tops, so it was useless to try. To take off on the river's edge was impossible, so there was only one solution - raft the plane back to the sandbar in midstream.

Ron, by this time had gone back to the University in Fairbanks, so Marvin, Charlie, and Art took on the project without him. With the large side door off the 206, they filled the plane with plastic liners from small barrels. Art settled into the back seat behind the liners, and in this manner they flew to the Kink where they got rid of their load. They chose a bog just a few hundred feet from the river, and as they made passes over it, Art pushed the liners out the open doorway.

Their next trip up there was with the Cub filled with small pieces of plywood and short boards they needed to build enough of a raft to hold the barrel liners together. Art thought he was going to have a second trip up into the Fortymile, but he couldn't fit into the space they had reserved for him. Charlie somehow was able to squeeze in. Three more Cub trips completed their airlift.

On their last trip, they assembled their raft with the plastic liners as floats, and loaded the plane on it, ready to be moved. By this time it was late fall and the water was low - not more than three feet deep. Halfway across the water from the bank to the bar, the raft was grounded, so they let it go down the river and pushed the plane the last half of its trip by hand. Here they put on a new prop, repaired the wingtip, and tied the plane down. The next day, Marvin and Ellis Roberts went back together in 32 Zulu, the same plane Ellis had used to bring our fishermen out from T Lake. They set down on the sand bar. With Marvin in the crippled plane

198

and Ellis in the other one, our two little Cubs cleared the bar and came home.

CHAPTER XXII

Business was always slow and life was apt to get dull along in January every year, so someone dreamed up the 600 race. This was a snow machine race that started in Anchorage in mid-January, and traveled six hundred miles through Glenallen, Tok, Delta, and on to Fairbanks. A bevy of reporters and photographers followed the race closely, and Union Oil furnished free fuel for all the racers. Cathedral Bluffs was one of their stops. The first race in 1969 created a lot of interest and drew a sizeable number of contestants. Temperatures dropped to minus fifty just in time for the race, and hung in there until it was over.

But that didn't discourage anyone. In 1970, we had our second and last 600 race. The morning the racers were to leave Tok, the Troopers blocked the road from Tok to Delta so the sno-go's would have clear sailing. We had five planes tied down in various places all around our buildings. One of the 180's was in a precarious position at the bottom of our driveway and close to the Union truck parked there to fill gas tanks. Marvin decided he had better get that plane at least out of the way and onto the airstrip before the snow machines started speeding in.

Charlie took his red flag down the road a block or so and Marvin taxied up the driveway, intending to make a right-hand swing onto the highway and then roll on down to the airstrip three hundred feet away. But when he tried to make his turn, he discovered his right brake was frozen. Art ran out to give his left wing strut a push and turn the plane. But just then a reporter from Fairbanks who hadn't been aware of the road block and didn't realize Charlie and the red flag were in the road for a purpose, came driving through from Tok. By the time he saw the wingtip of the plane, he was so startled he couldn't think what to do. Instead of staying in the middle of the road straight ahead, he made a sudden turn into our driveway. His car sashayed, hit the tail of the plane and threw it all the way across the highway into the other ditch, with the opposite wing hanging out over the road.

When Art realized the car wasn't stopping, he let go of the strut and started running, but he couldn't run fast enough. The fender hit him and threw him into the ditch. The car landed in a pile of rocks we had used to fill in a low spot beside our driveway. We had a real mess.

Marvin ran immediately down to the house to phone the Troopers.

"We've got a car and an airplane piled up out here at the end of our driveway. Can you come up?"

The Trooper on duty said, "I sure can't come right now, Marvin. I've got this whole town full of snow machines trying to get underway and I don't dare leave for a little while. Can you just take names and license numbers and clear the road off the best you can? I'll get there as soon as possible."

In the meantime, some of the race officials had been setting up their radio equipment and had some sawhorses and planks they had intended to use for road blocking just beyond Cathedral toward Fairbanks. They immediately got the blocking out right at the top of the hill, and we set up a barrel in the middle of the highway toward Tok, just in case someone else ran our flag.

The fellows decided they would push the airplane to the airstrip, but before they ever got a chance to get underway, a semi-truck came barreling up the hill from Fairbanks way. The driver saw the roadblock from the bottom of the hill, but somehow he said it didn't register with him that it really meant the highway was blocked. At the crest of the hill, he suddenly realized what was ahead, but it was too late to start braking. He crashed through the sawhorses, throwing planks in every direction, and laid on the horn. There was nothing else he could do. But he took the middle course. He hit just the wingtip of the plane on the right side, and missed the back end of the car by inches on the other side.

The reporter, realizing the truck wasn't making any effort to stop, jumped into the middle of the road to knock the barrel out of the way, but he never reached the barrel. Knowing there wasn't enough time, he jumped backwards again and barely cleared the front end of the truck. It hit the barrel, threw it into the air, and finally came to a stop two blocks down the road. The driver was one scared man. His truck wasn't damaged. So he left his name and license number and went on down the highway.

We finally got the plane into its parking place and tied down, put planks under the car to get it off the rock pile, and everyone congregated at the house for coffee.

"I thought when I saw that truck tearing down on us that I'd bought the farm," Marvin admitted. "I could just visualize a smashed plane, a smashed car, a smashed truck, and bodies all over the place."

The trooper finally arrived. Since he had done most of his flying with us and had made many a road landing on out-of-the-way places with Marvin, this was an unpleasant assignment for him. He cited Marvin for an unlicensed vehicle and the reporter for negligent driving. So with a smashed plane and a crippled car, we went on with the 600 race.

We were in a bad way as far as planes were concerned. All we had left to operate with were a Cessna 180 on skis, a 206 on wheels that Marvin didn't have a lot of faith in, and two Super Cubs that we had laid up during the cold weather. We had to replace that damaged 180 as fast as we could, because even in January there were some fields where you couldn't land with skis.

We made a lot of phone calls in the next few days, and closed a deal with someone in Houston who had an almost-new 180 in excellent condition. Marvin planned to fly out and pick it up himself if he could squeeze the trip in between mail runs and pacify RCA long enough to let him skip a trip out to the Gold King site.

But before he could leave, we had the small matter of appearing at at hearing before the magistrate in Tok.

Marvin had two flights that day of the hearing. He had Mike Molchan sitting up at Eagle waiting to come out and take his wolf pelts into Fairbanks. And it was mail day in Tetlin.

"I can fly to Eagle in the dark, just as long as I have light enough to land," he reasoned. So he was up long before daylight, and on his way. There wasn't going to be enough time to come all the way back home, so I met him with the pickup at the magistrate's office; and Mike and I sat through the hearing. The Trooper wasn't there that morning, so a young fellow we called Baby Face, fresh out of the academy in Sitka, sat in for him.

The hearing over, Marvin loaded his mail into the plane and started for Tetlin. Mike and I, in the pickup, headed for Cathedral Bluffs. But somewhere on the Tanacross flats a few miles out of Tok, the Trooper's car with Baby Face in it went past us at top speed and up into the hills just ahead. I remembered that someone in Tok had told us just before we pulled out of town that a car had gone in the ditch up there, so I slowed down a bit and took all the hills and corners cautiously.

Sure enough, right at the bottom of a low spot between two hills, with a curve on each side, sat the police car. Fifty feet off the road in brush and snow sat another car. Baby Face was just wading knee deep in snow back to the road with a young native boy in tow, already in handcuffs. He hailed us down and instructed me to pull up on the left side of the road, nose to nose with his car. I objected because I could just see another semi coming down one of those blind hills on either side of us, and plowing into my car parked on the wrong side of the road.

But the trooper insisted, because he said he needed assistance. On the spot he deputized me and gave me the job of guarding his prisoner while he went back to search the car for liquor.

Mike and I sat there while he frisked the kid, and instructed him to stand beside the trooper's car until he got his searching job done. Then he waded back through the snow to the stalled car, leaving his prisoner alone. The boy had no coat on, and the rest of us were dressed in parkas. We watched the fellow shiver, and finally he asked me if I would get a cigarette out of his breast pocket and light it for him.

"I don't think I can do it," I said. "I'm not sure just what I am supposed to do, but I doubt that I should come close to you.

204

If you'll just wait until you get into the Trooper's car, I'm sure he will let you smoke. Are you cold?''

"Yes I am!" He gave me a disgusted look, and right before our eyes he began to wiggle and maneuver his handcuffed wrists until he managed not only to pull a cigarette out of his pocket, but also got hold of a match and lit it! Mike and I sat there with our mouths open, astounded

Satisfied there was nothing in the car he wanted, Baby Face finally came back to the road.

"Can I go now?" I asked.

"Not just yet. I want you as a witness while I read him his rights."

So he hauled that poor kid over to the window of our car, pulled out a little book from his pocket, and began to read from it in legal lingo.

But he never finished. Just about that time we heard the hum of an airplane coming over the hills.

"Oh migosh!" I cried. "That's Marvin coming back from the mail run! If he sees me sitting here with a trooper by my car,...!''

The plane broke over the hill just at that moment. Marvin was right on top of us when he evidently recognized his own pickup sitting down there. He made an about turn, and swooped down over us to take another look.

Baby Face fell all apart. He slammed the book shut, pulled his prisoner back away from the car door and shouted above the roar of the plane, "Get going! Get going quick!"

Mike grunted his disgust, and we were on our way.

Marvin met us at the car door as soon as we pulled into Cathedral.

"So I'm not the only one who gets tickets!" he smiled a bit smugly. "What did you do wrong?"

I think he was actually a little disappointed when he found out what had really happened.

Getting to Fairbanks to catch a plane out to Houston was a problem. Cyndie had graduated from the University of Alaska the year before and was at the Unviversity of Michigan in Ann Arbor that winter, doing graduate work. Ron was just finishing up his last year at the University in Fairbanks. We had just the two younger boys at home with us.

I could go into town with Marvin, but I didn't want to drive that long way back by myself. The roads were narrow, crooked, and slippery. But neither did we want to take one of the boys with us and leave the other alone with a power plant and gas pumps to operate.

We had about made up our minds I would go without one of the boys when Mabel Scoby called from the Fortymile Roadhouse.

"There's a truck driver here on his way to Fairbanks. If Marvin can be ready in a half hour, he has a ride to town."

Marvin piled his bag, some rations, a sleeping bag and some heavy boots at the front door, greeted the driver like an old friend when he pulled up, and minutes later they were gone. Just like that.

His trip back from Houston was a rough one. He lost a day at that end of the trip because it came to light that the pilot he was buying the plane from owed some money on it yet. So they had to wait until the bank opened the next morning before they could get that matter straightened out. Then Marvin had to buck forty-five mile per hour headwinds all the next day. If he managed enough good weather to stay half of every day in the air, he was lucky. He spent most of one whole day over South Dakota making no progress at all because of storms he was trying to dodge, and backtracking when he couldn't dodge them.

Finally on his third day, he was able to sneak into Havre, Montana where he would go through customs. But there was no place he could get the plane into a hangar, and it was fifteen degrees below zero. Someone gave him a ride the five miles into town. By the time he had eaten a meal, he decided he didn't dare let the plane sit out all night because it would never start the next morning. Traffic had folded for the night and there were no cabs, so he walked back that five miles to the field and sat in the plane all night, starting the motor up every hour or so.

Weather was bad all the way to Edmonton, and by that time he had been on the way four days. He was already way past due and his scheduled flights piling up, so he phoned me to let me know I'd have to try to pacify RCA, and to see if either Bob or Ellis Roberts would do his mail run for him.

I picked up the mail at the post office the next morning and Ellis got it to Tetlin. We just assumed we wouldn't be seeing Marvin for another couple of days at least. Everyone else, including Floyd Miller who was the customs agent at Northway, thought the same thing. The FAA had been monitoring his progress all the way from Houston and knew where he was.

But weather must have changed drastically down through Canada, because late that afternoon we got a call from the station in Northway saying Marvin was already enroute from Whitehorse and would be landing at Northway in a half hour.

Floyd was making a hurry-up trip to Tok to pick up the Tetlin teachers and take them back to their village. With his 185 on wheels, he landed in deep snow at Tok, and flipped his plane. He ruined the prop and spinner and vertical stabilizer, broke a motor mount, and pushed the motor back against the firewall. Besides that, he wrinkled one wing right where the strut was fastened. So when Marvin arrived at Northway, there was no customs agent there. He waited a half hour or so, then began blustering around about how he didn't have to wait indefinitely to go through customs, and he was going to leave for home.

But Floyd didn't waste any time. He wife loaded a new prop into the car at Northway and was on the way to Tok with it minutes after the accident.

Everyone in Tok seemed to congregate at the airfield. The Utilities company had its truck there, so they pulled it up at the front of the plane to use as an anchor. Then with ropes tied on it in all directions and people at the end of every rope, they used Roberts' big cat to pull the plane back onto its wheels.

Floyd was a good pilot with a lot of spunk. He put on the new prop, had Ellis pull the plane from the field onto the highway with the cat, and flew it back to Northway. Marvin was still sitting there when he arrived. Floyd wheeled his damaged plane into the hangar, shut the doors, and without missing a beat, got out his paperwork and put Marvin through Customs.

At home that night Marvin gave us a blow-by-blow account of his trip to Houston.

"Did you get to Fairbanks in time to catch the plane out that night?" I asked.

"Oh yes. You know that truck driver took me right out to the airport and then stayed there until I had my ticket."

"That was sure nice of him to do all that for a stranger," I beamed.

"Oh, he wasn't a stranger," Marvin corrected me. "Didn't I introduce you to him? I thought you knew him. He was the fellow who drove the semi through all that mess out here the morning of the 600 race."

CHAPTER XXIII

It did look like a busy summer ahead. A big mining exploration crew was moving into the bunkhouse for the summer and wanted air support. Our first big job was to fly fuel in fifty-five gallon drums up into the Fortymile country for them. From then on, once they got a camp set up, it would be hauling in supplies and men. We were still doing the Gold King run twice a week, the mail run twice a week; and once fire season started, Marvin would be flying fire patrol every spare minute he had.

We put out some feelers for a pilot-mechanic, and one day we got a call from Fairbanks. Marvin talked to him for quite some time.

"I think," he said when he hung up the receiver, "that we've found our boy. It sounds as though this fellow is exactly what we need."

"Marvin," I began, "do you realize we've been at this rat race non-stop for fifteen years? Little did we dream back in '48 when you soloed over the hospital back in Menomonie what it was all going to lead up to. Have you added up your hours lately?"

"Yup. Almost twelve thousand just two days ago."

I did some fast mental totaling. "Fifteen years and twelve thousand hours! It's no wonder I feel tired."

"We're both getting tired out, Lou," Marvin agreed. "But this is going to be our last year. Charlie and Art will both be in college this fall and I don't see how we can operate here without them. The planes have gotten too big for you and me to beat around by ourselves. If we can just hang on until fall, maybe we can close up the operation and go south for the winter. We need it."

Yes, we were both tired. Fifteen years of rat race, with never a break. We hadn't been home in fourteen years, and we were homesick. This next year would be the first in sixteen that I hadn't been teaching the children by correspondence at home. All four of them had gone from kindergarten through senior high school in our own front room, with lessons recited at the dining room table. Now we were a few short weeks from the end, as both the younger boys were finishing up their senior year.

"You're right, Marvin," I agreed. "We'll hang tough this summer no matter what. This fall we'll go to the Bahamas - you talk about it every winter, but we never get there. I think the time has finally come."

Ron's draft number had come up in December, but he had a deferment until school was out in the spring. In the meantime, he and three other young men in the graduating class had signed up for the Air National Guard. They had gone to Anchorage for physicals, but all four of the medical reports got lost in the mail somewhere between Anchorage and Fairbanks.

Charlie, Art, and I went to town for graduation exercises that Monday during the third week in May, but Ron had been delegated to go to Anchorage to pick up the duplicate medical reports, so he stayed on at the dorm to fly to Anchorage the next day.

Thursday I went back to Fairbanks to bring home Ron and a whole pickup load of whatever it is that kids accumulate in a dorm room during four years of college. My biggest concern that day was his family of fish. He had two aquariums full of exotic fish plus heat lamps, pumps, and thermostats. Originally he had planned to donate it all to the biology lab, but Mary Roberts offered them a home, so we decided the fish would come to Tok. Transporting them meant putting them inside some big balloons full of water and then keeping them at room temperature until they could get back into their aquariums. It wasn't an easy job.

We had a real homecoming that night. Not only was this Ron's first trip home since Christmas, but Helen Foster and her co-worker, Florence Weber from Fairbanks, had both arrived.

210

Florence would be there for just a few days, but Helen for the whole summer.

Ron had done some flying that spring out of Fairbanks in a Cessna 172 he leased at Phillips Field. Marvin had never flown a 172, and I think it pleased him that his kid had one up on him. They sat at the counter in the cafe and did a lot of talking about it. Dan, a young pilot Marvin had hired, meeting Ron for the first time, sat by silently appraising this young man just three years his junior, and a possible competitor for his position in the family of pilots at Cathedral Bluffs.

Finally the boys all went to the house to set up the aquarium and get their pumps and heat lamps in operation. Marvin, Helen, and Florence planned their flying schedule for the next day, and then Marvin tagged the boys to the house to have a look at the living room full of goldfish.

We all got to bed late that night. "It's sure nice to have Ron home again," Marvin sighed as he pulled the blankets up around his ears. "I guess he really likes that 172. And you know he sounds as though his mind is all made up to go down to the University of Oregon next fall to do graduate work in water resources. That should be a good field. I just wish we could keep him at home this summer, but I guess kids have to...when the opportunity..." And so he drifted off to sleep.

He was still tired the next morning when I got up at six to feed a crew at seven o'clock.

"Mom, I don't think I'm going to make it," he groaned, and began to drag himself out of bed.

"Why don't you sleep in another half hour? You don't have to fly fire patrol until nine o'clock, and didn't you say Helen will wait for her flight until you get back from that?" But he started his day anyway.

Helen, Florence, and Dan were already at the counter and eating before Marvin had his plane checked out for the day's run and came in for breakfast. He ate in a hurry, stacked his dishes on the table behind me as he went through the kitchen, and from there on into the shop.

211

Seconds later it happened. One terrible deafening explosion, and then silence. Silence, that is, except for the steady putt-putt of the Witte power plant.

We all froze for an instant. I dropped my fork and spatula, and pushed into the shop. All I saw was utter devastation - the compressor was upside down in the middle of the floor, and an exploded paint pot lay on the work bench; white paint was splattered all the way from the ceiling to the floor, and at my feet Marvin lay motionless, terribly injured and bleeding. His whole head was a mass of white paint mixed with his own red blood. My world had come to an end.

The whole place came into action within seconds. Dan, an ex-Marine, was at Marvin's side, pulling out his tongue. Art, taking care of a gas customer, stopped in the middle of his pumping and came running to the shop, his customer right on his heels. Ron and Charlie, who were still in bed when the explosion came, were there not two minutes later. I had already called the Troopers and asked them to send the doctor and ambulance from Tok.

"He can never make it in an ambulance!" Ron announced. "We've got to have that big chopper the BLM has down at Tanacross!"

A quick call to the BLM office let us know the pilot and co-pilot were somewhere down in Tok eating breakfast. Helen and Florence started for Tok to locate them, and minutes later Ron and Art followed in the pickup to help speed up the search. Charlie stayed to help Dan and me. Marvin was in shock, and I covered him with blankets. There wasn't much else we could do for him.

We were twenty-five miles from Tok, but in an unbelievably short time the Trooper's car with Baby Face arrived. Right behind him came Dr. Miller from the Tok clinic, and behind him Bob McCarthy with the ambulance. Dr. Miller began immediately to prepare Marvin for his flight to the hospital.

One of the men from the car at the gas pump pushed his way into the shop. "I'm a pilot. If you want me to fly him in with your 185 sitting out here, I can do it!"

By this time Lavell Wilson, on his way to the RCA tower had stopped. He gave me the very slightest signal with his head, and I knew he wanted to talk to me. I followed him into the cafe.

"Don't let him do it," he whispered. "The fellow means well, but we can't take the chance. Don't know what kind of a pilot he is, and I don't think we can get the stretcher in the 185 without a lot of juggling. We'll wait for the chopper."

I knew someone had to make the trip with Marvin, and I assumed I would be the one to do it. I realized I had blood all over my shirt and that I had to change clothes, but my mind was a complete blank. I finally got into the bedroom and found a clean blouse. By the time I had changed, the chopper was setting down out at the end of the driveway, and men loading the stretcher into it.

Ron stopped me just as I was climbing in behind it.

"Mom, take good care of him!" he pleaded.

Suddenly I felt completely inadequate. "Ron, do you think you should go instead of me?" I almost hoped he would say yes, but he didn't.

"No. You go. Somebody's got to stay here and take care of things, too."

I squatted on the floor beside Marvin, as the chopper quivered, and started to rise. With the vibration of the machine, he began to slip off the edge of his pillow. I didn't dare touch that dear head all battered and swathed in bandages for fear of doing more damage, so I slid my hand under the edge of the pillow and eased it back into place.

Like I had sometimes imagined the plop plop of the old paddle wheels into the Yukon years ago, so sounded the constant plop plop of the chopper blades above our heads. Just as all our little silver airplanes had, over the years, cleared the trees at the end of the runway and shrunk steadily in size to a minature, and then a speck, Cathedral Bluffs too shrunk to a miniature, and then a speck, and finally became a part of the sky.

Where along the way, I wondered, had we slipped up? Why hadn't we finished the new roof we were putting on the lodge? Where was the retaining wall we had always planned to build? The swings for the kids? And whatever happened to the Bahamas?

See you later, Alligator!

But he never came back.

213

Epilogue

Marvin Warbelow passed away in Seattle on January 6, 1971, almost eight months after his accident. He never regained consciousness.

Ellis Roberts scattered his ashes over the area of the Kink where he had his last plane accident. The mountain that he, Helen, and Jo walked over on their way home has since been named Mt. Warbelow.

All four of our children now have families, and I have seven grandchildren. Cyndie and her husband have a general store, farm, and commercial greenhouses near Fairbanks.

Our three sons took over their father's air service. Charlie and Art still operate it under the name 40-Mile Air, Ltd. Ron eventually withdrew from the company and has his own helicopter service, Cassaron Helicopters, Ltd. The two businesses operate side by side with headquarters in Tok, Tanacross, and Fairbanks.